# Research Design

# Research Design

## Qualitative & Quantitative Approaches

# John W. Creswell

**SAGE** Publications
*International Educational and Professional Publisher*
Thousand Oaks   London   New Delhi

*For information address*:

SAGE Publications, Inc.
2455 Teller Road
Thousand Oaks, California 91320
E-mail: order@sagepub.com

SAGE Publications Ltd.
6 Bonhill Street
London EC2A 4PU
United Kingdom

SAGE Publications India Pvt. Ltd.
M-32 Market
Greater Kailash I
New Delhi 110 048 India


Printed in the United States of America

**Library of Congress Cataloging-in-Publication Data**

Creswell, John W.
    Research design: Qualitative and quantitative approaches / John
W. Creswell
        p.   cm.
    Includes bibliographical references and index.
    ISBN 0-8039-5254-6.   — ISBN 0-8039-5255-4 (pbk.)
    1. Social sciences—Research—Methodology.   2. Social sciences—
Statistical methods.   I. Title.
H62.C6963   1994
300'.72—dc20                                        94-4236


97  98  99  00  01  02  03  17  16  15  14  13  12  11

Sage Production Editor: Astrid Virding

▼

# *Acknowledgment*

To the hundreds of students in my doctoral level Proposal Development courses, I dedicate this book. I especially appreciate the inspiration to begin the project and the unflagging encouragement from Dr. Sharon Hudson. Dr. Leon Cantrell of Australia provided valuable services as a writer and conceptualist. Nette Nelson helped me visualize an overall format for the study and fine-tune its contents. Dr. De Tonack provided invaluable support in exploring the mixed-method studies. Dr. Ray Ostrander edited early drafts and helped develop the theory section. And Diane Greenlee edited and provided thoughtful guidance for the entire manuscript. Finally I am indebted to my family—Karen, David, and Johanna—for their support during the 3 years I worked on this book.

# ▼

# *CONTENTS*

# *ANALYTIC TABLE OF CONTENTS*

## Introduction to the Study

## The Purpose Statement

## Questions, Objectives, and Hypotheses

## The Use of a Theory

## Definitions, Delimitations, and Significance

## A Quantitative Method

▼

# *Preface*

## PURPOSE

This book advances a framework, a process, and compositional approaches for designing a qualitative or quantitative research study in the human and social sciences. With increased interest and use of qualitative research and with unclarity about its distinctive attributes from more traditional forms of research, this book offers a unique comparison of qualitative and quantitative approaches in the research process. This process includes deciding on a paradigm; using literature; writing an introduction; stating a purpose for the study; identifying research questions and hypotheses; using theory; defining, delimiting, and stating the significance of the study; and advancing methods and procedures for data collection and analysis.

## AUDIENCE

This book was written for graduate students and faculty who seek assistance in preparing a plan for a scholarly journal article, dissertation, or thesis. The book may be useful both as a reference book and as a text for graduate courses. To take best advantage of the design features in this book, the reader needs a basic familiarity with qualitative designs and quantitative research methods. However, terms are explained and recommended strategies are advanced for those needing introductory assistance in the design process.

## FORMAT

At each research phase, examples are shared from journal articles, dissertation proposals, and dissertations. Although my primary specialization is education, the illustrations presented draw broadly from human and social science fields. Chapter 4, for instance, includes examples from nursing, education, criminal justice, higher education, and psychology. I hope the reader will find breadth of exposure to broad fields of knowledge essential in the research process, such as the philosophical paradigms of social science research, quantitative research methods, qualitative research methods, dissertation proposal design and development, and writing and narrative techniques.

This book is not a detailed method text; it is a guide to major design decisions. Nor is it a comprehensive statement about the designs types, qualitative or quantitative. The quantitative approaches used as examples are surveys and experiments, frequently used designs in the human and social sciences. The qualitative approaches are ethnography, case studies, grounded theory, and phenomenology. Historical and legal research is omitted because of the extensive treatment of these types elsewhere. Additionally this book provides only an introduction to the philosophical assumptions of qualitative and quantitative paradigms of knowledge; readers are referred to more detailed accounts in other books and articles. Also, although students preparing dissertation proposals should find this book helpful, topics about negotiating a study with graduate committees are addressed thoroughly in other texts.

Consistent with accepted conventions of scholarly writing, I have tried to eliminate any words or examples that convey a sexist or ethnic orientation. Examples were selected to provide a full range of gender and cultural orientations. Moreover, in referencing citations in the examples, the reference list for this book includes only the original reference, not the entire list of references cited within quoted material. Interested readers can examine the original citation for references embedded within examples. Finally several features have been added to improve the readability of the manuscript: bullets to emphasize key points, boldface type, and numbers where steps are needed. An analytic table of contents provides reference to key points.

## OUTLINE OF CHAPTERS

This book is comprised of 11 chapters. The overall format in each chapter is to present principles about composing and writing qualitative and quantitative approaches and to illustrate these principles with specific examples. Moreover, these design principles are grounded in the paradigms assumptions of Chapter 1. Also in Chapter 1 are formats for designing an entire study. Writing exercises at the end of each chapter relate to these formats so that one can end the book with a written plan for a scholarly study.

Chapter 1, "A Framework for the Study," addresses a focus for the study; choosing a single paradigm for this focus—either qualitative or quantitative; considering the method of data collection and analysis within this paradigm; and identifying a methodology or format for the study (a *methodology* being defined here as the entire research process from problem identification to data analysis). Chapter 2, "Use of the Literature," also provides a foundation for the entire study plan. This chapter presents how and when to use literature in qualitative and quantitative studies, the purpose of a literature review, information about library resources, types of literature, and components of an article to be summarized in a

literature review. Also included is discussion about a research literature map for summarizing the literature.

With this foundation in the paradigm discussion and the literature, the discussion addresses the first section in an actual plan for
a study, "The Introduction to the Study." In Chapter 3 several
differences in writing the introduction from a qualitative and
quantitative standpoint are proposed, and a general social sciences
model is presented consisting of issue-problem-literature-audience
components. In Chapter 4, "The Purpose Statement," the importance of this statement is discussed first, followed by key principles
to be included in writing a purpose from a qualitative and quantitative perspective. After planning a general "purpose statement,"
researchers next design specific research questions, objectives, or
hypotheses. As discussed in Chapter 5, "Questions, Objectives, and
Hypotheses," key design principles are advanced for both paradigms,
and good models of composition are provided. In Chapter 6 the
"Use of a Theory" is addressed. This chapter begins with a definition of a theory and its characteristics and then presents information about using theory in qualitative or quantitative studies. In
Chapter 7, "Definitions, Delimitations, and Significance," the
components of defining terms, delimiting and limiting a study, and
stating the significance of a study for varied audiences are discussed. As with all of the chapters, design principles and examples
are integrated into the discussion.

Chapters 8, "A Quantitative Method," and 9, "A Qualitative
Procedure," convey information about data collection and data analysis for both paradigm perspectives. The objective here is not to
present a "method text," but to highlight key decisions that need to
be made in designing a study. Throughout these two chapters, other
texts are referenced to provide detailed discussion. Chapter 10,
"Combined Qualitative and Quantitative Designs," departs from
prior chapters in that the discussion presents design decisions for
**combining** qualitative and quantitative approaches in a **single**
study. After a brief sketch of the literature on triangulation, mixed
methods, and mixed design, the chapter includes three models for
combining designs: a two-phase model, a dominant-less dominant
model, and a mixed methodological design. All three models are
illustrated with examples from journal articles. In Chapter 11,

"Scholarly Writing," strategies are presented for the composition process, such as narrative voice, writing as thinking, the habit of writing, and coherence and readability. Then the discussion turns to editorial considerations—the active voice, strong verbs and nouns, and the "fat" in sentences. The chapter ends with thoughts about computer programs available for writing and editing.

Finally, designing a study is a difficult and time-consuming process. This book will not necessarily make the process easier, but it should provide comfort with the research process, enable one to better understand the paradigms in use, and explore the writing and composition process at work in scholarly research.

# 1

▼

# *A Framework for the Study*

The design of a study begins with the selection of a topic and a paradigm. Paradigms in the human and social sciences help us understand phenomena: They advance assumptions about the social world, how science should be conducted, and what constitutes legitimate problems, solutions, and criteria of "proof" (Firestone, 1978; Gioia & Pitre, 1990; Kuhn, 1970). As such, paradigms encompass both theories and methods. Although they evolve, differ by discipline fields, and often are contested (Phillips, 1987), two are discussed widely in the literature: the qualitative and the quantitative paradigms (Philips, 1987; Reichardt & Cook, 1979; Webb, Beals, & White, 1986). In this book a **qualitative study** is designed to be consistent with the assumptions of a qualitative paradigm. This study is defined as an inquiry process of understanding a social or human problem, based on building a complex, holistic picture, formed with words, reporting detailed views of informants, and conducted in a natural setting. Alternatively a **quantitative study**, consistent with the quantitative paradigm, is an inquiry into a social or human problem, based on testing a theory composed of variables, measured with numbers, and analyzed with statistical procedures, in order to determine whether the predictive generalizations of the theory hold true.

In this chapter I address the selection of a paradigm and a format for pursuing the methodology—the process of research—within the paradigm. First, however, one needs to begin by selecting a focus for the study.

## A FOCUS FOR THE STUDY

The *focus* for a study is the central concept being examined in a scholarly study. It may emerge through an extensive literature review, be suggested by colleagues, researchers, or advisors, or be developed through practical experiences.

▼ *Focus the topic by describing it succinctly, drafting a working title, and considering whether it is researchable.* In a single sentence try to describe the focus concisely. Complete the following sentence: "My study is about . . ." Possible responses: "My study is about at-risk children in the junior high," "My study is about helping college faculty become better researchers." At this stage in the design, frame the answer to the question so that another scholar might grasp easily the meaning of the project. A common shortcoming of beginning researchers is that they frame their study in complex and erudite language. This perspective may result from reading published articles that have undergone numerous revisions before being set in print. Good, sound research projects begin with straightforward, uncomplicated thoughts, easily read and understood.

Drafting a working title for the study will help focus the direction of research. Although some would suggest that the title be saved for last, I recommend a working draft at this time to position the central concept before the writer at an early stage. Undoubtedly this working title will be modified as one proceeds with a project.

Wilkinson (1991) provided useful advice for creating a title: Be brief and avoid wasting words. Eliminate unnecessary words such as "An Approach to . . ." and "A Study of . . ." Use a single title or a double title. An example of a double title: "An Ethnography: Understanding a Child's Perception of War." In addition to Wilkinson's thoughts, consider a title no longer than 12 words, eliminate most articles and prepositions, and make sure it includes the focus or topic of the study.

Next consider whether this topic is researchable. One needs criteria for making this decision. Below are questions often asked by individuals as they plan a study:

Is the topic researchable, given time, resources, and availability of data?

Is there a personal interest in the topic in order to sustain attention?

Will the results from the study be of interest to others (e.g., in the state, region, nation)?

Is the topic likely to be publishable in a scholarly journal? (or attractive to a doctoral committee?)

Does the study (a) fill a void, (b) replicate, (c) extend, or (d) develop new ideas in the scholarly literature?

Will the project contribute to career goals?

Before proceeding with a study, one needs to weigh these factors and to ask others for their reactions to a topic. Seek reactions from colleagues, noted authorities in the field, academic advisors, and faculty committee members and colleagues.

## A PARADIGM FOR THE STUDY

*The Two Paradigms*

Once one is comfortable proceeding with a specific focus, the next decision involves selecting an overall paradigm for the study. I present two choices—the qualitative and the quantitative—that have roots in 20th-century philosophical thinking.

The **quantitative** is termed the traditional, the positivist, the experimental, or the empiricist paradigm. The quantitative thinking comes from an empiricist tradition established by such authorities as Comte, Mill, Durkheim, Newton, and Locke (J. Smith, 1983). The **qualitative** paradigm is termed the constructivist approach or naturalistic (Lincoln & Guba, 1985), the interpretative approach (J. Smith, 1983), or the postpositivist or postmodern perspective (Quantz, 1992). It began as a countermovement to the positivist tradition in the late 19th century through such writers as Dilthey, Weber, and Kant (J. Smith, 1983).

*Assumptions of the Paradigms*

To understand the assumptions of each paradigm, writers have contrasted them on several dimensions (Firestone, 1987; Guba & Lincoln, 1988; McCracken, 1988). Although these contrasts are a heuristic device (seldom do actual studies exemplify all of the ideal characteristics of either paradigm), they bring into stark contrast the nature of alternative strategies (Patton, 1988). Table 1.1 displays assumptions of quantitative and qualitative paradigms based on ontological, epistemological, axiological, rhetorical, and methodological approaches. It is important to understand these assumptions because they will provide direction for designing all phases of a research study (in the chapters to follow).

On the **ontological** issue of what is real, the **quantitative** researcher views reality as "objective," "out there" independent of the researcher. Something can be measured objectively by using a questionnaire or an instrument. For the **qualitative** researcher, the only reality is that constructed by the individuals involved in the research situation. Thus multiple realities exist in any given situation: the

**Table 1.1**  Quantitative and Qualitative Paradigm Assumptions

| Assumption | Question | Quantitative | Qualitative |
|---|---|---|---|
| Ontological Assumption | What is the nature of reality? | Reality is objective and singular, apart from the researcher. | Reality is subjective and multiple as seen by participants in a study. |
| Epistemological Assumption | What is the relationship of the researcher to that researched? | Researcher is independent from that being researched. | Researcher interacts with that being researched. |
| Axiological Assumption | What is the role of values? | Value-free and unbiased | Value-laden and biased |
| Rhetorical Assumption | What is the language of research? | Formal<br>Based on set definitions<br>Impersonal voice<br>Use of accepted quantitative words | Informal<br>Evolving decisions<br>Personal voice<br>Accepted qualitative words |
| Methodological Assumption | What is the process of research? | Deductive process<br>Cause and effect<br>Static design—categories isolated before study<br>Context-free<br>Generalizations leading to prediction, explanation, and understanding<br>Accurate and reliable through validity and reliability | Inductive process<br>Mutual simultaneous shaping of factors<br>Emerging design—categories identified during research process<br>Context-bound<br>Patterns, theories developed for understanding<br>Accurate and reliable through verification |

SOURCE: Based on Firestone (1987); Guba & Lincoln (1988); and McCracken (1988).

researcher, those individuals being investigated, and the reader or audience interpreting a study. The qualitative researcher needs to report faithfully these realities and to rely on voices and interpretations of informants.

On the **epistemological** question, the relationship of the researcher to that being researched, the two paradigms also differ. The **quantitative** approach holds that the researcher should remain distant and independent of that being researched. Thus in surveys and experiments, researchers attempt to control for bias, select a systematic sample, and be "objective" in assessing a situation. The **qualitative** stance is different: Researchers interact with those they study, whether this interaction assumes the form of living with or observing informants over a prolonged period of time, or actual collaboration. In short, the researcher tries to minimize the distance between him- or herself and those being researched. This response has implications, too, for the **axiological** issue of the role of values in a study. The researcher's values are kept out of the study in a **quantitative** project. This feat is accomplished through entirely omitting statements about values from a written report, using impersonal language, and reporting the "facts"—arguing closely from the evidence gathered in the study. The major difference between this approach and that of the **qualitative** researcher is that the qualitative investigator admits the value-laden nature of the study and actively reports his or her values and biases, as well as the value nature of information gathered from the field. The language of the study may be first person and personal.

Another distinction is the **rhetoric,** or language of the research. When a **quantitative** researcher writes a study, the language should be not only impersonal and formal but also based on accepted words such as *relationship, comparison,* and *within-group.* Concepts and variables are well defined from accepted definitions. This orientation marks a quantitative study. Different words mark **qualitative** studies; authors of qualitative texts during the 1980s (e.g., Lincoln & Guba, 1985) constructed a language distinct from the traditional research language in order to emphasize the qualitative paradigm. Such words as *understanding, discover,* and *meaning* formed the glossary of emerging qualitative terms. Moreover, the language of qualitative studies became personal, informal, and based on definitions that evolved during a study.

From these distinctions about reality, the relationship between the researcher and that researched, the role of values, and the rhetoric of the study has emerged a **methodology**—the entire process of a study—that differs too. One approaches a **quantitative** methodology by using a deductive form of logic wherein theories and hypotheses are tested in a cause-and-effect order. Concepts, variables, and hypotheses are chosen before the study begins and remain fixed throughout the study (in a static design). One does not venture beyond these predetermined hypotheses (the research is context free). The intent of the study is to develop generalizations that contribute to the theory and that enable one to better predict, explain, and understand some phenomenon. These generalizations are enhanced if the information and instruments used are valid and reliable. Alternatively, in a **qualitative** methodology inductive logic prevails. Categories emerge from informants, rather than are identified *a priori* by the researcher. This emergence provides rich "context-bound" information leading to patterns or theories that help explain a phenomenon. The question about the accuracy of the information may not surface in a study, or, if it does, the researcher talks about steps for verifying the information with informants or "triangulating" among different sources of information, to mention a few techniques available.

### A Single Paradigm

▼ *Identify a* **single** *research paradigm for the overall design of the study.* Although in Chapter 10 I address combined paradigm designs, compelling reasons exist for a single paradigm at this time. Pragmatically, to use both paradigms adequately and accurately consumes more pages than journal editors are willing to allow and extends dissertation studies beyond normal limits of size and scope. By examining studies in journals that employ combined paradigms, one can see that they tend to be funded projects with multiple investigators collecting data over an extended period of time. Using both paradigms in a single study can be expensive, time-consuming, and lengthy

(Locke, Spirduso, & Silverman, 1987). Also researchers (and faculty) seldom are trained in the skills necessary to conduct studies from more than one paradigm; individuals learn one paradigm, and this perspective becomes the dominant view in their research.

### Criteria for Selection

How, then, does one choose between the qualitative and the quantitative paradigms? **Table 1.2** presents five criteria that illustrate factors to consider.

Researchers bring to a study a **worldview,** an outlook, that favors the qualitative or quantitative ontological, epistemological, axiological, rhetorical, and methodological assumptions. For example, some individuals see reality as subjective and want a close interaction with informants. Others may be more comfortable with an objective stance using survey or experimental instruments. Undoubtedly this worldview may be affected by a second factor—**training or experiences.** An individual trained in technical, scientific writing, statistics, or computer statistical programs and familiar with quantitative journals in the library would choose the quantitative paradigm. The qualitative approach incorporates much more of a literary form of writing than the quantitative approach. Library experiences with qualitative journals and texts are important to provide illustrations of good writing. With the advent of qualitative computer software programs, experience in using these, too, is an asset for those choosing the qualitative approach.

Another factor is **psychological attributes.** Because quantitative studies are the traditional mode of research, carefully worked-out procedures and rules exist for the research. In addition, collecting information and analyzing data from surveys or from instruments in an experimental design involve a shorter period of time than that required of qualitative designs. Hence a researcher who engages in a quantitative study seeks out this paradigm because it offers a low-risk, fixed method of research without ambiguities and possible frustrations. This researcher also would have a shorter time for the study. Alternatively the qualitative design is one in which the "rules" and procedures are not fixed, but rather are open and

**Table 1.2** Reasons for Selecting a Paradigm

| Criteria | Quantitative Paradigm | Qualitative Paradigm |
|---|---|---|
| Researcher's Worldview | A researcher's comfort with the ontological, epistemological, axiological, rhetorical, and methodological assumptions of the quantitative paradigm | A researcher's comfort with the ontological, epistemological, axiological, rhetorical, and methodological assumptions of the qualitative paradigm |
| Training and Experience of the Researcher | Technical writing skills; computer statistical skills; library skills | Literary writing skills; computer text-analysis skills; library skills |
| Researcher's Psychological Attributes | Comfort with rules and guidelines for conducting research; low tolerance for ambiguity; time for a study of short duration | Comfort with lack of specific rules and procedures for conducting research; high tolerance for ambiguity; time for lengthy study |
| Nature of the Problem | Previously studied by other researchers so that body of literature exists; known variables; existing theories | Exploratory research; variables unknown; context important; may lack theory base for study |
| Audience for the Study (e.g., journal editors and readers, graduate committees) | Individuals accustomed to/supportive of quantitative studies | Individuals accustomed to/supportive of qualitative studies |

emerging. This design calls for an individual who is willing to take the risks inherent in an ambiguous procedure. This person, too, needs to have time for a lengthy study, one requiring at least a year for data collection alone.

Whether certain "problems" are better suited for qualitative or quantitative studies is open to debate. However, the **nature of the problem** is an important factor, albeit only one on the list. For quantitative studies the problem evolves from the literature, so a substantial body of literature exists on which the researcher can build. Variables are known, and theories may exist that need to be tested and verified. For qualitative studies the research problem needs to be explored because little information exists on the topic. The variables are largely unknown, and the researcher wants to focus on the context that may shape the understanding of the phenomenon being studied. In many qualitative studies a theory base does not guide the study because those available are inadequate, incomplete, or simply missing.

A final factor is the **audience** for the research. A choice of paradigm must be sensitive to the audience, whether this audience consists of journal editors, journal readers, graduate committees, or colleagues in the field. The paradigm of choice must be one the audience understands or at least supports as a viable, legitimate methodology.

## METHODS ASSOCIATED
## WITH THE PARADIGMS

At this stage in the design, it is useful to consider the method for data collection and analysis to be associated with the paradigm of choice.

▼ *Identify a tentative guiding method for use within the qualitative or quantitative paradigm.* Consider **quantitative methods** as consisting of two types:

**Experiments** include true experiments with the random assignment of subjects to treatment conditions and quasi experiments that use nonrandomized designs (Keppel, 1991). Included within quasi experiments are single-subject designs.

**Surveys** include cross-sectional and longitudinal studies using questionnaires or structured interviews for data collection with the intent of generalizing from a sample to a population (Babbie, 1990).

In **qualitative** methods (or approaches) the human and social sciences offer several traditions. These traditions may be method types for data collection, analysis, and reporting writing, or overall designs that include all phases in the research process. Jacobs (1987), for example, discussed designs in human ethology, ecological psychology, holistic ethnography, cognitive anthropology, ethnography of communication, and symbolic interactionism. M. Smith (1987) categorized qualitative research into the interpretive approach, artistic approaches, systematic approaches, and theory-driven approaches. Tesch (1990) identified 20 types and categorized them into those addressing the characteristics of language, the discovery of regularities, the comprehension of meaning, and reflection. Lancy (1993) noted anthropological perspectives, sociological perspectives, biological perspectives, the case study, personal accounts, cognitive studies, and historical inquiry. McCracken (1988) advanced a historical sketch of the evolution of qualitative approaches from sociology, psychology, anthropology, evaluation research and administrative sciences, and consumer research.

To limit the types in this book, I cite examples from four designs frequently found in human and social science research:

---

**Ethnographies,** in which the researcher studies an intact cultural group in a natural setting during a prolonged period of time by collecting, primarily, observational data (Wallen & Fraenkel, 1991). The research process is flexible and typically evolves contextually in response to the lived realities encountered in the field setting (Grant & Fine, 1992; Spradley, 1979). Examples in this book are drawn also from **critical ethnography,** a style of discourse and analysis embedded within conventional ethnography. In this approach the researcher chooses between conceptual alternatives and value-laden judgments to challenge research, policy, and other forms of human activity (Thomas, 1993). Critical ethnographers attempt to aid emancipatory goals, negate repressive influences, raise consciousness, and invoke a call to action that potentially will lead to social change.

**Grounded theory,** in which the researcher attempts to derive a theory by using multiple stages of data collection and the refinement and interrelationship of categories of information (Strauss & Corbin, 1990). Two primary characteristics of this design are the constant comparison of data with emerging categories, and theoretical sampling of different groups to maximize the similarities and the differences of information.

**Case studies,** in which the researcher explores a single entity or phenomenon ("the case") bounded by time and activity (a program, event, process, institution, or social group) and collects detailed information by using a variety of data collection procedures during a sustained period of time (Merriam, 1988; Yin, 1989).

**Phenomenological studies,** in which human experiences are examined through the detailed descriptions of the people being studied. Understanding the "lived experiences" marks phenomenology as a philosophy based on the works of Husserl, Heidegger, Schuler, Sartre, and Merlau-Ponty (Nieswiadomy, 1993), as much as it is a method of research. As a method the procedure involves studying a small number of subjects through extensive and prolonged engagement to develop patterns and relationships of meaning (Dukes, 1984; Oiler, 1986). Through this process the researcher "brackets" his or her own experiences in order to understand those of the informants (Nieswiadomy, 1993).

## A FORMAT FOR COMPOSING SECTIONS

Assuming that one has a paradigm for the guiding methodology in the study and a method type within this paradigm, the next step is to conceptualize a format for the entire study.

▼ *Select a format for the overall design of the study.* The format for a **quantitative** study conforms to standards easily identified in journal articles and research studies. The form generally follows the model of an introduction, a literature review, methods, results, and discussion. In planning a **quantitative** study and designing a dissertation proposal, consider the following three-part format to sketch the overall plan:

*Example 1.* **Quantitative** *Format*

Introduction

    Context (Statement of the Problem)

    Purpose of the Study

    Research Questions or Objectives or Hypotheses

    Theoretical Perspective

    Definition of Terms

    Delimitations and Limitations of the Study

    Significance of the Study

Review of the Literature

Methods

    Research Design

    Sample, Population, or Subjects

    Instrumentation and Materials

    Variables in the Study

    Data Analysis

Appendices: Instruments

The plan shown in Example 1 is a standard format for a social science study, although the order of the sections, especially in the introduction, may vary from study to study (see Miller, 1991; Rudestam & Newton, 1992). It presents a useful model for designing the sections of a plan for a dissertation or sketching the topics to be addressed in a scholarly study.

The format is much less standardized in **qualitative** designs than quantitative designs. A fundamental characteristic, however, should be that the design is consistent with the qualitative paradigm assumptions. Moreover, with qualitative research relatively new on the landscape of human and social science research, the design ideally should convey a strong rationale for the choice of a qualitative design. In light of these points, I propose two alternative models: Example 2 is one I have used, and Example 3 is recommended by Marshall and Rossman (1989):

*Example 2.*  **Qualitative** *Format*

Introduction

    Statement of the Problem

    Purpose of the Study

    The Grand Tour Question and Subquestions

    Definitions

    Delimitations and Limitations

    Significance of the Study

Procedure

    Assumptions and Rationale for a Qualitative Design

    The Type of Design Used

    The Role of the Researcher

    Data Collection Procedures

    Data Analysis Procedures

    Methods for Verification

    Outcome of the Study and Its Relation to Theory and Literature

Appendices

*Example 3.*  **Qualitative** *Format (Marshall & Rossman, 1989)*

Introduction and General Questions or Topic

Significance of the Research

Site and Sample Selections

Researcher's Role in Management, Including Entry, Reciprocity, and Ethics

Research Strategies

Data Collection Techniques

Managing and Recording Data

Data Analysis Strategies

Management Plan, Timeline, Feasibility

Appendices

Although these two examples are similar, my model emphasizes more introductory topics, such as definitions, delimitations, and limitations, as well as information about the assumptions and specific design used in the study. Regardless of the differences, both models represent a reasonable format for a qualitative design.

## SUMMARY

In this chapter I focused on selecting a paradigm for a scholarly study. I addressed focusing a topic by using the techniques of scripting a single sentence that completes the thought, "My study is about . . . ," drafting a working title, and addressing whether the focus is researchable. I recommended choosing a **single** paradigm for the study, based on the distinctive characteristics of the qualitative and quantitative paradigm assumptions. These differences are the nature of reality (the ontological assumption), the relationship of the researcher to that being researched (the epistemological assumption), the role of values (the axiological assumption), the use of language and words (the rhetorical assumption), and the overall process of the research study (the methodological assumptions). The rationale for a **single** paradigm is based on such issues as time, skills, and the overall size of the project. I suggested that the rationale for the **paradigm of choice** be based on worldview or assumptions of each paradigm, training and experience, psychological attributes, the nature of the problem, and the audience for the study. Within a paradigm, one needs to specify the method used. Quantitative method types discussed in this book are surveys and experiments; qualitative method types (or designs) are ethnographies, grounded theory studies, case studies, and phenomenology studies. From the paradigm and the method type, one considers the methodology, the format for the entire study. Examples were provided of formats for designing quantitative and qualitative studies.

# WRITING EXERCISES

1. Draft a working title for your study. Use the suggestions advanced in this chapter for the design of the title. If preparing a dissertation or a thesis, prepare the title page for the study.

2. Develop a table of contents for the study, based on one of the formats presented in this chapter.

# ▼ ADDITIONAL READINGS

Firestone, W. A. (1987). Meaning in method: The rhetoric of quantitative and qualitative research. **Educational Researcher,** 16(7), 16-21.

William Firestone examines both a quantitative and a qualitative study of the same research question. He provides a clear discussion of the two methodologies and of their underlying assumptions. Further analysis shows the different uses of rhetoric in the two paradigms. Differences in the use of language and of presentation are linked to fundamental differences in the paradigms. An important conclusion is that although different in assumptions and methods, quantitative and qualitative research can be seen usefully as complementary, rather than rival, designs.

Guba, E. G., & Lincoln, Y. (1988). Do inquiry paradigms imply inquiry methodologies? In D. M. Fetterman (Ed.), **Qualitative approaches to evaluation in education** (pp. 89-115). New York: Praeger.

Egon Guba and Yvonna Lincoln provide axioms that distinguish between the conventional (positivistic) and the alternative (naturalistic) paradigms in the social sciences. These differences are the nature of reality, the relationship of the knower to the known, the outcomes of inquiry, the dynamics of action, and the role of values in inquiry. In addition they provide excellent visual renderings of the methodology of the conventional and naturalistic inquiry. The authors see these methodologies as "non-miscible in any proportion" (p. 111). And they advocate that methodologies are rooted in paradigms, and that researchers should be observant of the assumptions that undergird their research.

Howe, K., & Eisenhart, M. (1990). Standards for qualitative (and quantitative) research: A prolegomenon. **Educational Researcher,** 19(4), 2-9.

Kenneth Howe and Margaret Eisenhart emphasize that, as positivism is no longer a viable epistemological doctrine, the debate between qualitative and quantitative paradigms needs to focus on particular aspects of various research methodologies, rather than on abstract epistemology. They stress the importance of ensuring that the research questions drive the methodology, and not vice versa. Five general standards for educational research are (a) the fit between research questions and techniques of data collection and analysis, (b) the effective application of chosen techniques of data collection and analysis, (c) understanding of background assumptions, (d) overall warrant, and (e) value constraints; these underline the authors' perception of the importance and rigor of appropriate techniques, rather than methodological purity.

Marshall, C., & Rossman, G. B. (1989). **Designing qualitative research.** Newbury Park, CA: Sage.

Catherine Marshall and Gretchen Rossman outline the sections of a qualitative proposal: introduction, significance of the research, review of related literature, statement of the problem, research questions, focus of the study, and research design. This six-step plan for a design provides useful advice. In addition the authors offer a clear guide to the steps involved in justifying the use of qualitative research methods. They stress the importance of demonstrating how research design emerges from a consideration of the methodological literature. The section on proposal format offers useful advice on how qualitative proposals might address concerns of positivist researchers.

Rudestam, K. E., & Newton, R. R. (1992). *Surviving your dissertation.* Newbury Park, CA: Sage.

Kjell Rudestam and Rae Newton provide readers with advice on the entire dissertation process, such steps as selecting a topic, conducting a literature review, presenting tables and figures, working with faculty committees, and addressing writing issues. They also advance a section on methods of inquiry wherein they identify the characteristics of qualitative and quantitative approaches to educational research. They provide many useful tables, such as a table on differences among statistical tests, and tables on how to present analysis from SPSS statistical procedures. This book is an excellent guide for doctoral dissertation and master's thesis students.

Salomon, G. (1991). Transcending the qualitative-quantitative debate: The analytic and systemic approaches to educational research. **Educational Researcher,** 20(6), 10-18.

Gavriel Salomon argues that the debate emphasizing the quantitative-qualitative dichotomy obscures the inherently complementary nature of the two approaches. He proposes alternative sets of assumptions—the analytic and the systemic—as a more useful way of thinking about complementary differences in research paradigms and methods. The analytic approach describes the assumptions and methods appropriate to precision and measurement; the systemic approach stresses authenticity and flux. No single paradigm or set of assumptions is necessarily superior to the other. It is important to select what is most clearly a function of the particular aspect or unit of the world one wishes to study. Complementing research paradigms and methods means more than coexistence; it underlines how one approach can inform and guide the other.

Tuckman, B. W. (1990). A proposal for improving the quality of published educational research. **Educational Researcher,** 19(9), 22-25.

Bruce Tuckman argues that far too much published research in education has serious deficiencies, ranging from substance to method. Existing strategies of manuscript evaluation are clearly inadequate. Tuckman proposes the adoption of a research evaluation framework (REF) in order to better assess manuscripts and offer technical guidance to authors. The proposed REF would have 30 criteria across nine topical areas: problem, literature review, hypotheses, design methodology, manipulations and measures, statistics, results, discussion, and write-up. Each criterion would be rated on a 5-point scale. Design methodology would have the highest weight (six criteria), and hypotheses the lowest (two criteria). The overall quality of a piece of research would be measured by its total score across all nine areas. Worksheets would provide evaluators with subsidiary questions, and necessary evaluator training materials would be provided. The REF could be adapted to allow the evaluation of qualitative research. A call is made for the American Educational Research Association to sponsor the REF proposal.

# 2
▼

# *Use of*
# *the Literature*

In this chapter I continue the paradigm discussion with a focus on planning the use of literature in a scholarly study. I begin by addressing the general purpose for using literature in a study and then turn to principles helpful in designing the use of literature in qualitative and quantitative studies. Finally design techniques, useful in planning, writing, and locating literature, regardless of paradigm, are advanced.

## PURPOSES OF THE LITERATURE

The literature in a research study accomplishes several purposes: (a) It shares with the reader the results of other studies that are closely related to the study being reported (Fraenkel & Wallen, 1990). (b) It relates a study to the larger, ongoing dialogue in the literature about a topic, filling in gaps and extending prior studies (Marshall & Rossman, 1989). (c) It provides a framework for establishing the importance of the study, as well as a benchmark for comparing the results of a study with other findings. All or some of the reasons may be the foundation for writing the scholarly literature into a study (see Miller, 1991, for a more extensive discussion of purposes for using literature in a study). Beyond the question of *why* it is used is the additional paradigm issue of *how* it is used. I return to the paradigm discussion presented in Chapter 1 as a framework.

## THE LITERATURE IN A QUALITATIVE OR QUANTITATIVE STUDY

In **qualitative** research the literature should be used in a manner consistent with the methodological assumptions; namely, it should be used inductively so that it does not direct the questions asked by the researcher. One of the chief reasons for conducting a qualitative study is that the study is exploratory; not much has been written about the topic or population being studied, and the researcher seeks to listen to informants and to build a picture based on their ideas.

As with the use of theory, however, the amount of literature varies by type of qualitative design. In theoretically oriented qualitative studies such as ethnographies or critical ethnographies, the literature on a cultural concept or a critical theory from the literature is introduced by researchers early in their study plan. In grounded theory, case studies, and phenomenological studies, literature will be less used to set the stage for the study.

These two fundamental ideas—the inductive process of research and the variation in use of literature by design type—raise the question of where one should plan to use the literature in a qualitative study. I offer three placement locations, and the literature can be used in any or all of these locations. As shown in Table 2.1, one can discuss the related literature in the *introduction* to a study. It provides a useful backdrop for the problem—who has written about it, who has studied it, who has indicated the importance of studying the issue. This "framing" of the problem is, of course, contingent on available studies. One can find illustrations of this model in many qualitative studies employing different design types. The second form is to review the literature in a *separate section*, a model that resembles the more traditional form of conducting **quantitative** research. This approach is used most frequently when the audience consists of individuals or journals with a positivist orientation. Moreover, the theory-oriented qualitative studies, such as ethnography and critical theory, might locate the theory discussion and literature in a separate section, typically toward the beginning of the study. In the third form, the researcher may incorporate the related literature in the *final section* of the study, where it is used to compare and contrast with the results (or themes or categories) to emerge from the study. This model is especially popular in grounded theory studies, and I recommend it because it uses the literature inductively.

**Quantitative** studies include a substantial amount of literature to provide direction for the research questions or hypotheses. In planning a quantitative study, the literature often is used to introduce a problem in the introduction; is described in detail in a section titled "Related Literature" or "Review of Literature" or some other similar concept; and typically is advanced as a basis for comparing with results to be found in the study. Regardless of the placement, the literature is used deductively as a framework for the research questions or hypotheses.

A separate section on the review of the literature deserves special mention because it is a popular form for writing literature into a study. This literature review may take several forms, and no consensus exists about which form is preferable. Cooper (1984) suggested that literature reviews can be **integrative** where they simply are summaries of past research. This model is popular in dissertation proposals and dissertations. A second form recommended by Cooper is a **theoretical** review, wherein the researcher focuses on extant theory that relates to the problem being studied. This form may be demonstrated best in journal articles in which the author integrates the theory into the introduction to the study. A final form

**Table 2.1**   Criteria and Method Type for Using Literature in a Qualitative Study

| Use of the Literature | Criteria | Examples of Suitable Method Types |
|---|---|---|
| The literature is used to "frame" the problem in the introduction to the study. | Some literature must be available. | Typically used in all qualitative studies, regardless of type. |
| The literature is presented in a separate section as a "review of the literature." | This approach is often acceptable to an audience most familiar with the traditional, positivist approach to literature reviews. | This approach is used with those studies employing a strong theory and literature background at the beginning of a study, such as ethnographies, critical theory studies. |
| The literature is presented in the study at the end; it becomes a basis for comparing and contrasting findings of the qualitative study. | This approach is most suitable for the "inductive" process of qualitative research; the literature does not guide and direct the study, but rather becomes an aide once patterns or categories have been identified. | This approach is used in all types of qualitative designs, but it is most popular with grounded theory, wherein one contrasts and compares his or her theory with other theories found in the literature. |

23

suggested by Cooper is a **methodological** review, in which the researcher focuses on methods and definitions. These reviews may provide not only a summary of studies but also an actual critique of the strengths and weaknesses of the method sections. Some authors use this form in dissertations and in "review of related literature" sections in journal articles.

My suggestions, then, for planning to use the literature in a qualitative or quantitative study are as follows:

▼ *In a* **qualitative** *study use the literature sparingly in the beginning of the plan in order to convey an inductive design unless the qualitative design type requires a substantial literature orientation at the outset.*

▼ *Consider the most appropriate place for the literature in a* **qualitative** *study and base the decision on the audience for the project.* Keep in mind placing it at the beginning to "frame" the problem, placing it in a separate section, and using it at the end of a study to compare and contrast with the findings.

▼ *Use the literature in a* **quantitative** study deductively as a basis for advancing research questions or hypotheses.

▼ *Use the literature to introduce the study, to describe related literature in a separate section, and to compare with findings in a* **quantitative** *study plan.*

▼ *If a separate review of the literature is used, consider whether the literature will be described as integrative summaries, theoretical reviews, or methodological reviews.* A typical practice in dissertation writing is to advance an integrative review.

## DESIGN TECHNIQUES
## IN LITERATURE USE

Regardless of whether one is writing the literature into a qualitative or a quantitative study, several approaches are useful in identifying, writing, planning, and locating literature in a study.

*Material to Include in a Review*

▼ *Include essential information from articles in a review of a single research study or essay.* Researchers need to consider what material is to be extracted from a research study and summarized in a "review of related literature" section. Knowing what to abstract and how to abstract it quickly becomes an important issue when one is reviewing hundreds of studies. A good summary of a journal article includes the following points:

Mention the problem being addressed.

State the central purpose or focus of the study.

Briefly state information about the sample, population, or subjects.

Review key results that relate to the study.

Depending on whether or not the review is a methodological review (Cooper, 1984), point out technical and methodological flaws in the study.

In well-crafted journal articles, the problem and purpose statements are clearly stated in the introduction to the article. Information about the sample, population, or subjects is found midway through the article in a method (or procedure) section. The results often are reported toward the end of the article. For book-length research studies, look for the same points. Consider the following example:

*Example 1.   Review of a Quantitative Study*

In this example I present a paragraph summarizing the major components of a quantitative study (Creswell, Seagren, & Henry, 1979) much like the paragraph might appear in a "review of the literature" section of a dissertation or a journal article. In appearance the summary may look like an abstract, but in reality I consciously have chosen key components to address:

Creswell, Seagren, and Henry (1979) tested the Biglan model, a three-dimensional model clustering 36 academic areas into hard or soft, pure or applied, life or nonlife areas, as a predictor of chairpersons' professional development needs. Eighty department chairpersons located in four state colleges and one university of a Midwestern state participated in the study. Results showed that chairpersons in different academic areas differed in terms of their professional development needs. On the basis of the findings, the authors recommended that those who develop in-service programs need to consider differences among disciplines when they plan for programs.

I began with an "in-text" reference in accord with the format in the American Psychological Association style manual, **Publication Manual of the American Psychological Association** (American Psychological Association, 1984). Next I reviewed the central purpose of the study, followed by information about the data examined. I ended by stating the major results of the study and presented the practical implications of these results.

What about studies that are not research studies, but essays, opinions, typologies, and syntheses of past research? The material to be extracted from these nonempirical studies is as follows:

Mention the problem being addressed by the article or book.

Identify the central theme of the study.

Identify the major conclusions related to this theme.

If the review type is methodological, mention flaws in reasoning, logic, force of argument, and so forth.

Consider the following example:

*Example 2.  Review of a Study Advancing a Typology*

Sudduth (1992) completed a quantitative dissertation in political science on the topic of the use of strategic adaptation in rural hospitals. He reviewed the literature in several chapters at the beginning of the study. In an example of summarizing a single study advancing a typology, Sudduth summarized the problem, the theme, and the typology:

> Ginter, Duncan, Richardson, and Swayne (1991) recognize the impact of the external environment on a hospital's ability to adapt to change. They advocate a process that they call environmental analysis which allows the organization to strategically determine the best responses to change occurring in the environment. However, after examining the multiple techniques used for environmental analysis, it appears that no comprehensive conceptual scheme or computer model has been developed to provide a complete analysis of environmental issues (Ginter et al., 1991). The result is an essential part of strategic change that relies heavily on a non-quantifiable and judgmental process of evaluation. To assist the hospital manager to carefully assess the external environment, Ginter et al. (1991) have developed the typology given in Figure 2.1. (Sudduth, 1992, p. 44)

*A Priority for Reviewing the Literature*

▼ *I recommend that one establish a priority for one's search.* What types of literature might be reviewed and in what priority? Consider the following:

1. Begin with journal articles in respected, national journals, especially those that report research studies. By research I mean that the author or authors pose a question or hypothesis, collect data, and try to answer the question or support the hypothesis. Begin with single studies and move on to syntheses on topics. Start with the most recent studies about the topic and then work backward in time.

2. Next review books related to the topic. Begin with research monographs that are summaries of the scholarly literature. Then consider entire books that are on a single topic or that contain chapters written by different authors.

3. Follow this search by reading recent conference papers on a topic. Often conference papers report the latest research developments. Look for major, national conferences and the papers delivered at them. Most major conferences either require or request that authors submit their papers for inclusion in computerized indices.

4. If time permits, especially at the dissertation proposal stage, look at the abstracts of dissertations in **Dissertation Abstracts International** (University Microfilms, 1938-). Dissertations vary immensely in quality, and one needs to be selective in examining these studies. But a search of the **Abstracts** might result in one or two relevant dissertations. Once these dissertations are identified, request copies of them through interlibrary loan or through the University of Michigan Microfilm Library.

I placed journal articles first on the list because they are the easiest to locate and duplicate. They also report the "research" about a topic. Dissertations are listed last because they vary considerably in quality and are the most difficult reading material to locate and reproduce.

A final word needs to be mentioned about networking with other researchers around the country. Make contact with authors of studies. Seek them out at conferences. Write or phone them to ask whether they know of studies related to the proposed study and whether they have an instrument that can be used or modified to measure variables.

*A Model for Delimiting*
*the Literature Review*

When composing a review of the literature, it is difficult to determine how much literature to review. To address this problem, I have developed a model that provides parameters around the literature review, especially as it might be designed for a quantitative study or a qualitative study that employs a standard literature review section.

▼ *Write a review of the literature that contains sections about the literature related to major independent variables, major dependent variables, and studies that relate the independent and dependent variables.* This approach seems well suited for dissertations and for conceptualizing the literature to be introduced in a journal article. Consider a literature review (in a dissertation or proposal) to be composed of five components: an introduction, Topic 1 (about the independent variable), Topic 2 (about the dependent variable), Topic 3 (studies that address both the independent and dependent variables), and a summary.

1. Introduce the section by telling the reader about the sections to be found in the literature review. This passage is a statement about the organization of the section.

2. Review Topic 1, which addresses the scholarly literature about the **independent** variable or variables. With several independent variables, consider subsections or focus on the single most important variable. Remember to address only the literature about the independent variable; keep the literature about the independent and dependent variables separate in this model.

3. Review Topic 2, which incorporates the scholarly literature about the **dependent** variable or variables. With multiple dependent variables, write a subsection about each variable or focus on a single, important dependent variable.

4. Review Topic 3, which includes the scholarly literature that relates the **independent** variable(s) to the **dependent** variable(s). Here we are at the crux of the proposed study. Thus this section should be relatively short and should contain studies that are extremely close in topic to the proposed study. If nothing has been written on the topic, construct a section that is as close as possible to the topic, or review studies that address the topic at a general level.

5. Provide a summary of the review, highlighting the most important studies and capturing major themes in the review.

This model focuses the literature review, relates it closely to the variables in the research questions and hypotheses, and sufficiently narrows the study. It becomes a logical point of departure for the method section.

## A Research Map of the Literature

One of the first tasks for a researcher working with a new topic is to organize the literature about the topic. This task enables a person to understand how his or her study of the topic adds to, extends, or replicates research already completed.

▼ *A useful tool for this task is to design a map of the research literature.* Maps are visual renderings of the literature, and they can be organized in different ways. The central idea is that the researcher begins to build a visual picture of existing research about a topic. Although maps can be created differently, one approach is to draw a map by first stating the topic to be researched—what would capture in a word or two the key idea presented in the working title developed in Chapter 1? For **quantitative** studies this idea will be the key dependent variable in the study; for **qualitative** studies it will be the central focus or phenomenon being explored. For example, in a quantitative study the dependent variable might be "class size and instruction" or "organizational effectiveness." The map would present research studies about this topic. For example, in mapping the literature on "organizational effectiveness" one might find groups of studies: one group on issues in measuring this concept, another on correlates that influence it, and a third on definitions of the term. A visual rendering of the literature on organizational effectiveness could be made by presenting studies from the more general groups of studies to more specific studies. What would be the implications of this map?

---

The author could use this map as a visual picture of the literature that would help summarize literature already completed on the topic.

The author could write a box into this map to show how his or her study relates to the larger body of literature. The box showing the study to be undertaken might extend past studies, fill in a gap, or replicate past research. Such a map with a box can be a useful planning device and presentation schema for dissertation proposal presentations.

---

I next show two maps to illustrate this approach. Figures 2.1 and 2.2 show two different conceptualizations of maps. Figure 2.1 is a map from a **quantitative** project about the outdoor science education program in Nebraska (Locke, 1991). The author chose to track his progress through the literature by beginning with studies about a "definition of outdoor education." The second map, Figure 2.2, is an illustration of my preliminary analysis of studies about mixed-

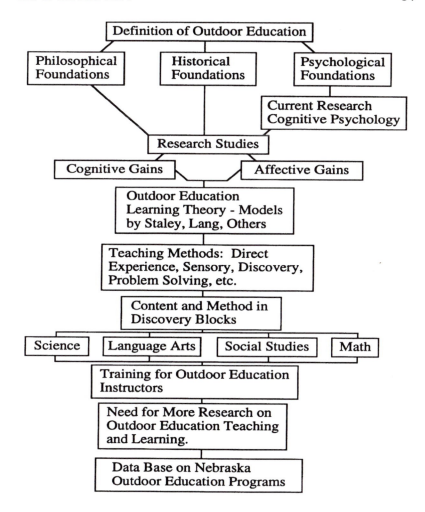

**Figure 2.1.** Locke's Research Map of the Literature

SOURCE: From *Nebraska's Outdoor Education Programs* [unpublished proposal] by W. Locke, 1991, University of Nebraska, Lincoln. Used with permission.

method designs (later reported in Chap. 10 of this book). I chose to identify topic areas in the literature about mixed-method designs, indicate key studies, and place my own study (or theme) within the existing literature. Notice that I drew a box around my study, along with lines to the respective literature that I wanted to extend.

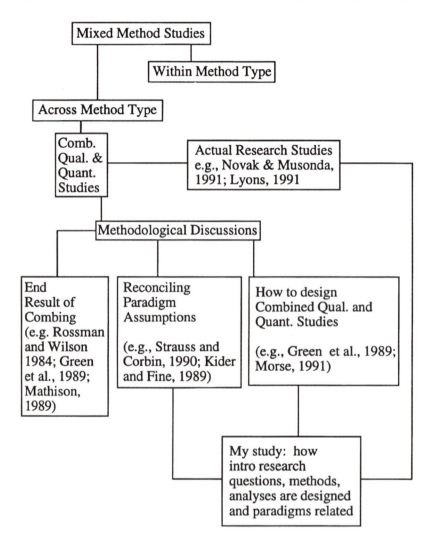

**Figure 2.2.** Creswell's Research Map on Mixed Method Studies

*Computerized Databases*

The development of a research map, of course, is predicated on finding the literature. Information retrieval has become the next frontier of scientific development for social and human science researchers. The Knowledge Navigator, for example, under development by Apple Computer, Inc., is a virtual library and resource world where one needs only to address a voice-sensitive notebook computer with natural language questions to receive exactly the information needed (Mitchell & Saunders, 1991). With a modem, a telecommunications software program, and a microcomputer, one can access the hundreds of available on-line public access catalogs (OPACs) from one's home office (see Schuyler, 1992, for a guide to these catalogs) by using Internet lists such as *Internet—Accessible Library Catalogs and Databases* or the National Science Foundation's *Internet Resource Guide* (Mitchell & Saunders, 1991). Internet is a worldwide, interconnected university, business, military, and science network (LaQuey, 1993). The academic library on campus, once offering an on-line mediated search of computerized databases by a reference librarian, now provides such easy access that researchers can scan the databases and Internet themselves.

Library holdings can be scanned quickly by using the computerized on-line catalog system. A survey of academic libraries reported that 98% of 119 academic research libraries had their bibliographic records of books and journals "on-line" for computer accessing (Krol, 1993). With Internet, catalog holdings of libraries across the country are also available. An example is the CARL (Colorado Association of Research Libraries) system in Colorado. It provides a wide assortment of on-line text, indices of model school programs, on-line book reviews, facts about the metropolitan Denver area, and a database on environmental education (Krol, 1993).

Libraries now can purchase CD-ROM from a vast array of databases (Finlay & Mitchell, 1991) and allow researchers to load the databases and retrieve citations to references. Although individuals may, in the near future, be able to access these CD-ROMs from their offices or home computers by using telecommunications, many research libraries have user stations in the libraries for accessing databases. Several databases commonly are used in research libraries.

The ERIC (Educational Resources Information Center) system is available on CD-ROM, and it provides complete access to many research studies. ERIC has two parts: CIJE, the **Current Index to Journals in Education** (Educational Resources Information Center,

1969-), and RIE, the **Resources in Education** (Educational Resources Information Center, 1975-). To best use the ERIC CD-ROM system, it is important to identify appropriate "descriptors" for the topic. This identification can be done by a search through a dictionary of terms, the **Thesaurus of ERIC Descriptors** (Educational Resources Information Center, 1975). But a random search through the **Thesaurus** may be time-consuming and futile. Alternatively a researcher might use the following procedure:

1. Look through the subject index found at the back of each CIJE and RIE. Look for a research study as similar as possible to the project being planned.
2. Examine the descriptors being used for that article. Select the major descriptors.
3. Use these major descriptors in the computer search. In this way, one uses the definition of descriptors being used by those who catalog articles for the ERIC system, which, in turn, maximizes the possibility of locating articles relevant for the planned study.

The **Social Sciences Citation Index (SSCI)** (Institute for Scientific Information, 1969-) is also available on CD-ROM. The SSCI is especially useful if one has a reference to a key study written some years ago. The SSCI enables one to trace all studies since the publication of the key study that have cited the work. Using this system, the researcher can develop a chronological list of references that document the historical evolution of an idea or a study.

Another CD-ROM database is **Dissertation Abstracts International** (University Microfilms, 1938-). In a full literature review for a dissertation, all sources, including the **Dissertation Abstracts,** need to be searched. Look for a few good dissertations from respected institutions that address a topic as close as possible to the topic under study.

Two more CD-ROM databases deserve special mention. *Sociological Abstracts* (1952-present) are available on CD-ROM called Sociofile. Sociological Abstracts is co-sponsored by the American Sociological Association, Eastern Sociological Society, International Sociological Association, and Midwest Sociological Society; it provides abstracts covering a broad range of sociological articles in periodicals in various languages (Sheehy, 1986). PsycLit, the CD-ROM for *Psychological Abstracts,* is the most popular CD-ROM database in academic research libraries (Tenopir & Neufang, 1992). *Psychological Abstracts* (1927-present) provides a bibliography listing new books, journal articles, technical reports, and other scientific documents in 16 major categories.

In summary, my recommendation is as follows:

▼ *Use computerized resources available through telecommunications or on-line user systems in libraries.*

*Style Manuals and*
*Bibliographic Citation Generators*

A basic tenet in reviewing the literature is to use an appropriate and consistent reference style. When sources first are identified in the literature, record them by using an accepted style. For dissertation proposals, graduate students should seek guidance from faculty, dissertation committee members, or department or college officials about the appropriate style for scholarly writing.

The **Publication Manual of the American Psychological Association** (APA, 1984) is used widely in education and psychology. The University of Chicago Press (**The Chicago Manual of Style,** 1993), Turabian (Turabian, 1973), and Campbell and Ballou (1977) also are used widely in the social sciences. Some journals even have developed their own variation of these popular styles. I recommend the following:

▼ *Adopt a style manual early in the planning process and identify one that is acceptable to the writing audience.* In addition, some of the most vexing style problems arise in the following instances:

When writing **in-text** references, keep in mind the appropriate form for types of references and pay close attention to the format for multiple citations.

When writing the **end-of-text** references, note whether the style manual calls for them to be alphabetized or numbered. Also cross-check that each in-text reference is included in the end-of-text list.

The **headings** are ordered in a scholarly paper in terms of levels. First note how many levels of headings are used in the paper. Then refer to the style manual for the appropriate format for the number of levels.

If **footnotes** are used, consult the style manual for their proper placement. Footnotes are used less frequently in scholarly papers today than a few years ago. But if they are included, note whether they go at the bottom of the page or at the end of the paper.

**Tables** and **figures** have a specific form in each style manual. Note such aspects as bold lines, titles, and spacing in the examples given in the style manual. In summary, the most important aspect of using a style manual is to be consistent in the approach throughout the manuscript.

▼ *Consider using computer bibliographic citation programs to help format references, especially when planning studies of dissertation length or when anticipating the publication of a study in several journals.* They enable a person to change style types quickly, as well as to organize efficiently hundreds of references. Many commercial programs are available; one I especially like and have used is **WP Citation** (Oberon Resources, 1990). This program works in conjunction with **Word Perfect 5.1** (WordPerfect Corporation, 1989). The researcher enters information for each citation in the order specified by **WP Citation** and creates a database. The type of information and order of entering information differs by publication (e.g., a book, an article). After all of the references are typed into this system, the merge program of WP5.1 is used to format the references into the exact format for the style specified. **WP Citation** now contains more than 400 reference formats. With such variety, researchers can convert their references quickly and accurately into several formats for different journals and audiences.

## SUMMARY

Researchers use the scholarly literature in a study to present results of similar studies, to relate the present study to the ongoing dialogue in the literature, and to provide a framework for comparing results of a study with other studies. Writing the literature into a qualitative study differs from writing it into a quantitative study.

The qualitative approach uses the literature inductively toward the end of a study; the quantitative approach uses it inductively at the beginning. Although I recommended placing the literature toward the end of a qualitative study (to be compared and contrasted with the outcomes of the study), it also can be found in the introduction to "frame" the problem or in a separate section called the "review of the literature." A common format for a quantitative study is to present a separate "review of the literature."

Useful design techniques, regardless of paradigm, are to summarize key components from a research study. These are the problem being addressed, the central purpose, information about the sample or subjects, and the key results. For an essay or a theoretical study, summarize the problem, the central theme, and the major conclusions. Consider a priority for searching the literature, beginning with the most respected, national refereed journal articles that report research studies. This search should be followed by books, conference papers, and dissertations. In addition, a model for delimiting a literature review (e.g., in a "review of the literature" section) would be to base the review on studies written about the independent variable, the dependent variable, and those studies that relate the independent to the dependent variable. A map of the literature can provide a useful visual that not only shows studies related to the topic being studied but also indicates how the present study relates to the larger literature.

To identify the literature, the computerized library systems can be helpful. Consider the on-line catalog and the CD-ROM databases available in many academic research libraries. One final design consideration is to identify an accepted style manual, given the audience for the study, and to consider using a computer bibliographic citation system systematically to organize and retrieve references in different styles.

# WRITING EXERCISES

1. Develop a visual map of the literature related to your topic.

2. If conducting a quantitative study, organize a "review of the literature" and follow the model for delimiting the literature to reflect the variables in the study.

3. If conducting a qualitative study, identify the literature that will be used to substantiate the problem being addressed in your proposed study. Summarize the major points of the studies.

4. If conducting a qualitative study, summarize the major studies that you likely will compare with the outcome of your qualitative investigation.

## ▼ ADDITIONAL READINGS

Fraenkel, J. R., & Wallen, N. E. (1990). **How to design and evaluate research in education.** New York: McGraw-Hill.

Jack Fraenkel and Norman Wallen outline six essential steps in preparing a review of the literature: (a) defining the research problem as precisely as possible, (b) perusing the secondary sources, (c) selecting and perusing an appropriate general reference, (d) formulating search terms, (e) searching the general references for relevant primary sources, and (f) obtaining and reading the primary sources and noting and summarizing key points in the sources. The key points to be summarized when reviewing an article are the problem, the hypotheses, the procedures, the findings, and the conclusions. In addition to these tips, Fraenkel and Wallen also provide an extensive discussion about using the ERIC system and conducting a computerized ERIC search.

Locke, L. F., Spirduso, W. W., & Silverman, S. J. (1987). **Proposals that work: A guide for planning dissertations and grant proposals** (2nd ed.). Newbury Park, CA: Sage.

Lawrence Locke, Waneen Spirduso, and Stephen Silverman describe 15 steps in the process of developing a review of literature. These 15 steps involve three stages: (a) developing the concepts that provide the rationale for the study, (b) developing the subtopics for each major concept, and (c) adding the most important references that support each subtopic. This entire process is presented visually with a research map and a specific illustration. One step in the process is to evaluate the "related literature" section by using questions about organization, headings, inclusiveness of the review, uniqueness of the study, and the use of major, key references.

Merriam, S. B. (1988). **Case study research in education: A qualitative approach.** San Francisco: Jossey-Bass.

Sharan Merriam provides an extensive discussion about the use of literature in qualitative studies. The literature review can help in the formulation of the problem, in the selection of methodology, and in the interpretation of research results. Merriam suggests that the literature review in a qualitative study is less prominent than in a deductive, theory-testing study. The researcher should become generally familiar with studies, but not review the literature extensively before data collection and analysis. The literature can be used to (a) describe the problem, (b) review previous work, and (c) present and interpret a study's results. A discussion of the study's findings might incorporate references to other reports and indicate how the study's findings deviate from previous work or support it.

# 3

▼

# *The Introduction*
# *to the Study*

With a focus for a study, a paradigm, an overall format for the study, and a literature review, one turns to the design of the introduction to a study. In this chapter I discuss the composition and writing of an introduction for a qualitative or quantitative study. I first build on the paradigm discussion in Chapter 1 by identifying minor distinctions between introductions written within the two paradigms. These distinctions are based on rhetorical, ontological, and methodological differences. Then I include a complete introduction as an example of a good model. This model is used to illustrate four key components in writing an introduction, regardless of paradigm: (a) establishing the problem leading to the study, (b) casting the problem within the larger scholarly literature, (c) discussing deficiencies in the literature about the problem, and (d) targeting an audience and noting the significance of the problem for this audience. Because this approach relies on stating the deficiencies of past literature, it is called the social sciences "deficiencies" model for an introduction.

## AN INTRODUCTION

An *introduction* is the first passage in a journal article, dissertation, or scholarly research study. It sets the stage for the entire study. As Wilkinson (1991) mentioned: "The introduction is the part of the paper that provides readers with the background information for the research reported in the paper. Its purpose is to establish a framework for the research, so that readers can understand how it is related to other research" (p. 96).

The introduction is difficult to write because it must address multiple objectives. It must (a) create reader interest in the topic, (b) establish the problem that leads to the study, (c) place the study within the larger context of the scholarly literature, and (d) reach out to a specific audience. All of these need to be accomplished within several pages of text. Therefore introductions are difficult to write, and many alternative structures are found in the scholarly journals. The four components of the introduction presented in this chapter hold true whether one writes a qualitative or a quantitative study. The content that one includes in the introduction, however, will differ slightly, depending on the paradigm. Relating the introduction back to Chapter 1, I discuss these differences in the paradigm assumptions.

## QUALITATIVE AND QUANTITATIVE INTRODUCTIONS

Earlier I said that the two paradigms differ in terms of the use of language and words. One difference is in the **point of view** used by authors in introductions to qualitative and quantitative studies. *Point of view* refers to the "point from which the action of the narration is viewed" (Brooks & Warren, 1961, p. 208). To determine the point of view, one must ask, Who tells (or is telling) the story?

and What is your relationship (as a writer) to the action? In planning a study, one should consider the different audiences and their requirements for point of view (Polyson, Levinson, & Miller, 1982).

A writer has three choices for his or her point of view (Hodges & Whitten, 1977):

---

The writer is the one speaking. Thus the first person point of view, and the writer uses the personal pronouns *I* or *we* in the introduction.

The writer is speaking to the reader. This approach is the second person point of view, and the writer uses the personal pronoun *you* in the introduction.

The writer is telling about the action. The third person point of view is being used, and the author writes impersonally from an omniscient view. A personal pronoun such as *it* may be used.

---

Researchers commonly use the more literary point of view of first or second person in **qualitative** studies. Personal pronouns such as *I, we,* and *you* may be written into the introduction. These points of view convey a personal, informal writing stance that lessens distance between the writer and the reader (a qualitative epistemological stance). A **quantitative** introduction typically is written from the third person point of view. This impersonal view removes the writer from the picture and helps create a sense of objectivity and distance between the researcher and that being researched (a quantitative epistemological stance).

The rhetorical differences also may be found in verb tense and types of questions. In a **qualitative** study, researchers often employ the present tense to connote immediate, direct action, or the past tense in a **quantitative** study to create distance between the written study and the action on which the study is based. Further, a **qualitative** study may employ more questions to guide the reader, whereas a **quantitative** study would not use questions and would be written in a more formal compositional style.

Another paradigm distinction is how one views the nature of reality (the ontological assumption) and the logic of one's design (inductive to deductive); it will shape the composition of the introduction. More specifically, it will affect how the literature and theory are used. From an ontological **qualitative** perspective, literature and theory are less apparent in an introduction because the researcher holds the worldview that "realty is socially constructed through individual or collective definitions of the situation" (Firestone, 1987, p. 16). In this perspective the qualitative researcher does not want to foreclose the debate by operating within tight strictures of past studies or literature. As Fetterman (1989) said about ethnographic qualitative research, "The ethnographer enters the field with an open mind, not an empty head" (p. 11). Moreover, the logic of the design (the methodology) will be inductive, developing a story or patterns from detailed categories or themes. This logic also suggests an emerging design, not a static design, wherein the categories develop during the study, rather than are predetermined before the study begins.

From a qualitative case study perspective, Merriam (1988) noted, "While a literature review helps in problem formulation regardless of design, its prominence in inductive research may be considerably less than in theory-testing studies" (p. 63). A grounded theory perspective from Glaser (1978) also supports an inductive approach: "In our approach we collect the data in the field first. Then start analyzing it and generating theory. When the theory seems sufficiently grounded and developed, then we review the literature in the field and relate the theory to it through the integration of ideas" (p. 31). But not all qualitative researchers are of a single mind about the inductive nature of an introduction. As in the case of the use of literature (mentioned in Chap. 2), some qualitative designs use a deductive approach to an introduction—employing a theory to be examined or tested in the introduction. Ethnographic studies from cultural anthropology, for example, include a strong cultural theory at the beginning of the study (Spradley, 1979); this format is especially so with critical theory studies. Thomas (1993) suggested that "critical researchers begin from the premise that all cultural life is in constant tension between control and resistance" (p. 9). This theoretical orientation shapes the structure of an introduction. In the introduction to her article, Beisel (1990), for example, proposed to examine how the theory of class politics explained the lack of success of an anti-vice campaign in one of three American cities. Thus, within some qualitative studies, the approach in the introduction may be less inductive and emerging while still relying on the perspective of an informant as in most qualitative studies.

Less variation is seen in **quantitative** introductions. Researchers assume that "there are social facts with an objective reality apart from beliefs of individuals" (Firestone, 1987, p. 16). An objective model, theory, or body of literature exists that begs for testing or exploration. One builds an extensive literature review in the introduction, setting the project firmly within a body of related literature. The writer tries to convey how the project will extend, fill a void in, or replicate this literature. As a result the literature review in the introduction will be more in-depth than the review in a qualitative study.

My suggestions for writing an introduction sensitive to the two paradigms are as follows:

▼ *Use the first or second person point of view in a* **qualitative** *study and the third person in a* **quantitative** *study.*

▼ *Write in a more literary style using present tense and questions in a* **qualitative** *study; write in a more formal style using past tense in a* **quantitative** *study.*

▼ *Make sure the introduction in a* **qualitative** *study conveys an inductive, emerging design, unless one uses the more theory oriented qualitative designs such as an ethnography or critical theory.* Use the literature to provide a rationale for the problem. *In a* **quantitative** *study, use a more deductive, static design where the literature and theory help direct the study.*

## AN ILLUSTRATION

With the paradigm assumptions in mind, the next step is to write an introduction. Although no single structure exists for a good introduction, I suggest that one consider a traditional social science model that I call the "deficiencies" model. I first present an entire introduction and emphasize in boldface type my interpretation of the author's intent. These interpretations then are discussed in detail in later sections of this chapter. My example is a quantitative study (Terenzini, Pascarella, & Lorang, 1982), "An Assessment of the Academic and Social Influences on Freshman Year Educational Outcomes." The example demonstrates major components that I discuss later:

> As the costs of higher education continue to rise, colleges and universities, whether public or private, are increasingly under pressure to document the consequences or outcomes of the educational programs and services they offer. (**Authors provide a narrative hook.**) Over the years, a considerable number and variety of claims have been made by the higher educational community regarding the direct and indirect benefits of college attendance, and legislators, taxpayers, parents and students are now beginning to ask to see the evidence supporting those claims. The evidence exists, but it is often of uneven quality, focusing in greater detail on certain educational impacts than on others.
> **(Authors describe a problem.)**
> Lenning, Munday, Johnson, Vander Well and Brue (1974a), for example, provide an entire volume of annotated references to studies addressing issues related to grades, academic persistence and academic learning. Their literature review indicates that a variety of background characteristics (e.g., socioeconomic status, educational level of parents, high school and geographic factors), personal traits (e.g., ability to handle stress, motivation, attitudes and values), activities and social interests, and instructional environment and programs have all been reliably related to various measures of grade performance, academic learning or continued enrollment. In a second (even larger) volume, these same authors (Lenning, Munday, Johnson, Vander Well & Brue, 1974b) reference a host of studies exploring the non-intellective correlates of other forms of collegiate success (e.g., personality development, social growth, or aesthetic-cultural development). Feldman and Newcomb (1969), of course, have also published an excellent review of the literature describing the outcomes of college.

**(Authors describe the literature about the problem.)**

Taken together, these reviews suggest several generalizations about the state of our knowledge concerning the impacts of college on students. First, the majority of these studies rarely involves more than one or two predictor variables, relying on univariate statistical procedures or, less frequently, on factorial analysis of variance designs. Thus, we know that a considerable number and variety of variables are related to equally numerous and various college impacts, but we have comparatively little basis for judging the relative importance among them.

Second, a significant number of the multivariate studies that have been done involved exploration of the sources of influence of some set of measures on a single outcome (dependent measure). Few studies have attempted to explore the simultaneous but differential impact of the same set of predictor variables on multiple outcomes. The work of Astin (1977) is a notable exception.

Third, the preponderance of studies focus on the personal traits of the students and their influence on educational outcomes. Sex, race, high school achievement, academic aptitude, personality characteristics and similar individual traits are common predictors. Far fewer studies have attempted to assess the relation between the developmental progress of students and the various collegiate experiences or programs presumed to influence that growth and over which institutions have some control. In short, a good deal is known about how students grow in the collegiate setting, but far less is known about the *institutionally induced* forms of student development.

Finally, as Lenning et al. (1974a, 1974b) noted, a disturbingly large number of the available studies were done without controlling for academic aptitude and other traits or background characteristics that students bring with them to college. The absence of controls creates interpretive problems both for studies focusing on the importance of individual traits and for those seeking to isolate institutional effects. In the former, the role of the trait(s) under investigation is commonly confounded by the influence of other, uncontrolled, student characteristics. In studies of institutional influences, failure to control for students' pre-college characteristics means that one cannot reject the hypothesis that students performed or grew as they did because of what they were like when they first matriculated. Even fewer studies test for the interaction of background and college experience variables, for the possibility that the same set of experiences or programs may have a differential effect on students with different traits. (**Authors mention deficiencies in the literature.**)

Thus, for college administrators, the question is less one of whether students change or grow in various ways during the college years than of whether (and how much of) the growth or change is attributable to the collegiate experience. Moreover, the issue is not really one of what the influences are, but rather of what the *institutionally controllable* influences are that have a positive effect on desirable educational outcomes. (**Authors target an audience.**) (pp. 86-89; reprinted by permission of *The Review of Higher Education*)

## THE PROBLEM IN THE STUDY

Terenzini et al. (1982) start with a general issue to which a wide readership can identify, and proceed to discuss a distinct problem: People now are beginning to ask for the evidence of the consequences or outcomes of educational programs. Clearly, from the authors' experiences and the evidence in the literature, a problem exists in colleges that needs to be researched.

Also note the first sentence in this opening paragraph by Terenzini et al. (1982). Is it a sentence that creates reader's interest? Is it a topic with which a wide readership can identify? The authors pose a good **narrative hook** (a term drawn from English composition) to draw the reader into the study. A study of first sentences would be a useful exercise for the aspiring researcher. Journalists provide good examples in their lead sentences to newspaper and magazine articles; the lead sentences in scholarly journal articles also illustrate good models. Here are a few examples of lead sentences from social science journals:

> "The transsexual and ethnomethodological celebrity Agnes changed her identity nearly three years before undergoing sex reassignment surgery." (Cahill, 1989, p. 281)

"Who controls the process of chief executive succession?" (Boeker, 1992, p. 400)

"There is a large body of literature that studies the cartographic line (a recent summary article is Buttenfield 1985), and generalization of cartographic lines (McMaster 1987)." (Carstensen, 1989, p. 181)

All three of the above examples present information easily understood by many readers. The first two, qualitative introductions, demonstrate how reader interest can be created by use of reference to the single informant and by posing a question. The third example, a quantitative-experimental study, shows how one can begin with a literature perspective. All three examples demonstrate well how the lead sentence can be written so that the reader is not taken into a detailed morass of thought, but rather is lowered gently into the topic.

I use the metaphor of the writer lowering a barrel into a well. The **beginning** writer plunges the barrel (the reader) into the depths of the well (the article). The reader sees only unfamiliar material. The **experienced** writer lowers the barrel (the reader, again) slowly, allowing the reader to acclimate to the study. This lowering of the barrel begins with a **narrative hook** of sufficient generality that the reader understands (and can relate to) the topic.

After the lead sentence, Terenzini et al. (1982) then discuss the problem leading to their study: They suggest that the evidence on outcomes of educational programs is of uneven quality and focus on some outcomes more than others. This step relates to writing the **problem** that the study addresses.

In applied social science research, problems arise from issues, difficulties, and current practices. For example, schools may not have implemented multicultural guidelines; the standards of faculty in colleges are such that they need to engage in professional development activities in their departments; minority students need better access to universities; a community needs to better understand the contributions of its early female pioneers. These are all significant problems that merit further study and establish a practical problem that needs to be addressed. McMillan and Schumacher (1989) suggested that research problems arise from deductions from theory, related literature, current social and political issues, practical situations, and personal experiences. A **problem**, then, might be defined as the issue that exists in the literature, theory, or practice that leads to a need for the study. By asking oneself, What is the rationale for the study? the problem begins to become clear.

The first paragraph or two of the introduction needs to establish the problem or issue that leads to the study. Keep the following essential points in mind as the "problem" is presented and composed:

▼ *Write an opening sentence that stimulates interest as well as conveys an issue to which a broad readership can relate.*

▼ *Specify the problem (dilemma, issue) leading to the study.* What issue establishes a strong rationale or need to conduct the study?

▼ *Indicate why the problem is important.*

▼ *Focus the problem statement on the key concept being tested quantitatively or explored qualitatively.* In a quantitative study this concept is the dependent variable; in a qualitative study it is the central phenomenon of interest.

▼ *As a general rule, refrain from using quotes in the lead sentence.* This rule may be relaxed in the case of **qualitative** studies written from a literary style.

▼ *Stay away from idiomatic expressions or trite phrases* (e.g., The lecture method remains a "sacred cow" among most college and university instructors).

▼ *Consider numeric information for impact* (e.g., Every year an estimated 5 million Americans experience the death of an immediate family member).

▼ *Consider short sentences for impact.*

## LITERATURE ABOUT THE PROBLEM

After establishing the problem in the first paragraph, Terenzini et al. (1982) next discuss the literature that has addressed student outcomes. Their paragraphs do not review single, isolated studies; instead they introduce entire volumes of research. The authors cast the problem within the larger literature about factors likely to contribute to student outcomes.

▼ *Discuss the literature that addresses the problem and set the problem within the ongoing dialogue in the literature.* Marshall and Rossman (1989) talked about setting a study "within a tradition of inquiry and a context of related studies" (p. 31). The ability to frame the study in this way separates the novices from the more experienced researchers. The veteran understands what has been written about a topic or certain problem in the field. This knowledge comes from years of experience in following the development of problems and their accompanying literature.

A reader needs to know what research has been written about the problem. Research can be defined in various ways. I define a "research" study as one that advances a research question and reports data to answer the question. If no "research" can be found, as indeed may be the case when one studies a narrow topic, the investigator can review literature broadly related to his or her topic. I use an inverted triangle to describe this phenomenon. At the apex of the inverted triangle lies the scholarly study. It is narrow and focused. If one broadens the review of the literature out to the base of the triangle, literature can be found, though it may be related only indirectly to the study at hand. This broad-based literature is reviewed to cast the problem within the literature.

Refer to the literature by summarizing groups of studies (unlike the focus on single studies in the integrated review in Chap. 2), not individual studies. The intent should be to establish broad areas of research at this juncture in the study. To de-emphasize single studies, place the in-text references at the end of a paragraph or at the end of a summary point about several studies.

## DEFICIENCIES IN PAST LITERATURE

After advancing the problem and casting the problem within the literature, the researcher needs to identify **deficiencies** in this larger literature. Certainly this model is not the only one in social science research; some studies seek to replicate other studies, suggesting that past work needs to be tested further. The larger literature is discussed, then, within the framework of a need to replicate studies. Other investigations attempt to discover something new because no one has explored the topic. This passage of the study then becomes a discussion about the need to go beyond the thoughts in the larger literature, to extend them.

When writing from a deficiencies approach, I suggest that one consider two points:

▼ *Write about areas overlooked by past studies, including topics, special statistical treatments, and significant implications.*

▼ *Discuss how the present study addresses these deficiencies and provides a unique contribution to the literature.*

These points might be written in a series of short paragraphs that identify three or four shortcomings of the past research, as was modeled by Terenzini et al. (1982). Alternatively one might focus on a single shortcoming and discuss how past research has overlooked or bypassed it.

In the two examples below, the authors point out the gaps or shortcomings of the literature. Notice their use of key phrases to indicate the shortcoming: "what remains to be explored," "little empirical research," and "very few studies."

*Example 1.   Deficiencies in the Literature*

For this reason, the meaning of war and peace has been explored extensively by social scientists (Cooper, 1965; Alvik, 1968; Rosell, 1968; Svancarova & Svancarova, 1967-68; Haavedsrud, 1970). What remains to be explored, however, is how veterans of past wars react to vivid scenes of a new war. (Ziller, 1990, pp. 85-86)

*Example 2.   Deficiencies in the Literature*

Despite an increased interest in micropolitics, it is surprising that so little empirical research has actually been conducted on the topic, especially from the perspectives of subordinates. Political research in educational settings is especially scarce: Very few studies have focused on how teachers use power to interact strategically with school principals and what this means descriptively and conceptually (Ball, 1987; Hoyle, 1986; Pratt, 1984). (Blase, 1989, p. 381)

## THE AUDIENCE

All good writers have the audience in mind. Terenzini et al. (1982) end their introduction by mentioning "college administrators" (p. 88) and the question these individuals might be asking themselves.

▼ *End the introduction by discussing the significance of the problem for a specific audience.* This can be accomplished through a short phrase or a longer passage. Moreover, comments might be addressed to a diverse audience of practitioners, other researchers, or policymakers. I also like the approach taken by Terenzini et al. (1982): to phrase a question that the audience likely would want to answer. This approach makes the study immediate and focuses the reader's attention on the central problem once again.

## SUMMARY

In this chapter I provided advice about composing and writing an introduction to a scholarly study. I suggested that one consider writing an introduction consistent with the assumptions of the paradigm used in a study. The language needs to consider the point of view of a first, second, or third person, the verb tense, and the use of questions. The logic of the design needs to consider whether the literature and theory will be used in an inductive, emerging design (qualitative) or in a deductive, static design (quantitative).

Then consider writing the introduction by using a standard social science "deficiencies" model. This model contains four parts: (a) state the problem or issue leading to the study and begin this opening paragraph with a narrative hook to which the reader can identify, (b) review the literature about the problem, (c) indicate the deficiencies in this literature, and (d) target the audience.

# WRITING EXERCISES

1. Draft several examples of narrative "hooks" for the introduction to the study and share these with colleagues to determine whether the hooks present an issue to which readers can relate.

2. Write the introduction to your proposed study. Include paragraphs setting forth the problem in the study, the related literature about this problem, the deficiencies in the literature, and the audience that would find the study of interest.

# ▼ *ADDITIONAL READINGS*

Bem, D. J. (1987). Writing the empirical journal article. In M. P. Zanna & J. M. Darley (Eds.), **The compleat academic: A practical guide for the beginning social scientist** (pp. 171-201). New York: Random House.

Daryl Bem emphasizes the importance of the opening statement in published research. He provides a list of rules of thumb for opening statements, stressing the need for clear, readable prose and for a structure that leads the reader step by step to the problem statement. Examples are provided of both satisfactory and unsatisfactory opening statements. Bem calls for opening statements that are accessible to the nonspecialist, yet not boring to the technically more sophisticated reader.

Merriam, S. B. (1988). **Case study research in education: A qualitative approach.** San Francisco: Jossey-Bass.

Sharan Merriam identifies three basic types of research problems: conceptual, action, and value. *Conceptual problems* arise from two juxtaposed elements that are conceptually or theoretically inconsistent. *Action problems* arise when a conflict offers no clear choice or alternative course of action. *Value problems* come from undesirable consequences. Merriam offers advice on how to observe and locate such problems, especially through the questioning of issues emanating from the everyday world.

Wilkinson, A. M. (1991). **The scientist's handbook for writing papers and dissertations.** Englewood Cliffs, NJ: Prentice Hall.

Antoinette Wilkinson identifies the three parts of an introduction: (a) the derivation and statement of the problem and a discussion of its nature, (b) the discussion of the background of the problem, and (c) the derivation and statement of the research question. She offers numerous examples of these three parts, together with a discussion of how to write and structure the introduction. Emphasis is placed on ensuring that the introduction leads logically and inevitably to a statement of the research question.

# 4
▼

# *The Purpose Statement*

The introduction focuses on the problem leading to the study, but it is the *purpose statement* that establishes the direction for the research. In a journal article the purpose statement commonly is written into the introduction; in a dissertation and a dissertation proposal it stands as a separate section. Because of its significance in a study, this entire chapter focuses on the purpose statement. This statement captures, in a single sentence or paragraph, the essence of a study. For this reason it should be written as clearly and concisely as possible. Moreover, like all components of the research process, it needs to be grounded firmly in the paradigm assumptions discussed in Chapter 1. In this chapter I address the reason for developing purpose statements, advance key principles to use in designing them, and provide examples to illustrate good models.

## SIGNIFICANCE AND MEANING
## OF A PURPOSE STATEMENT

According to Locke et al. (1987), the purpose statement should provide "a specific and accurate synopsis of the overall purpose of the study" (p. 5). Method and proposal-writing texts give scant attention to the purpose statement; they incorporate it into discussions about other topics. For example, Wilkinson (1991) refers to it within the context of the research question and objective; Fraenkel and Wallen (1990), as part of the research problem; and Castetter and Heisler (1977), within the statement of the problem. When one closely examines the content of these passages, each reference describes the central, controlling idea in a study. For this discussion I call the description of this idea "the purpose statement" because it conveys the overall intent or purpose of a study. As introduced in the prior chapter, the problem of the study is conveyed through an introduction. In the chapter to follow I address the writing of research questions and objectives, a topic that deserves attention in its own right.

The construction of a good purpose statement is based on the paradigm of study. Qualitative and quantitative purpose statements address similar content, but their precise form and language differ because of the rhetorical and methodological distinctions of each paradigm.

## A QUALITATIVE PURPOSE STATEMENT

A fundamental characteristic of a good **qualitative** purpose statement is that it implies or expresses the assumptions of the qualitative paradigm, such as the language of qualitative research (Firestone, 1987) and the methodology of an emerging design based on experiences of individuals in a natural setting (Merriam, 1988). Thus one might consider several basic design features of writing this statement:

▼ *Use such words as* purpose, intent, *and* objective *to call attention to this statement as the central controlling idea in a study.* Set off the statement as a separate paragraph and use the rhetoric of research by employing such words as "The purpose (or intent or objective) of this study is (was or will be) . . . " The present or past verb tense often is used in journal articles and dissertations; the future tense is used in dissertation proposals because researchers are presenting a plan for a study.

▼ *Use words that convey an emerging design because of the inductive mode of the research process in qualitative designs.* Such words as *describe, understand, develop, and discover* convey this sense.

▼ *Eliminate words in the purpose statement that suggest a directional orientation to the study* (e.g., successful, informing, useful). Also refrain from using such words as *relationship* or *comparison*, which convey a **quantitative** cause and effect or group comparison methodology. By eliminating these words, the researcher conveys an open, evolving stance in the design. McCracken (1988) referred to the need in qualitative interviews to let the respondent describe his or her experience. Interviewers (or purpose statement writers) violate the "law of nondirection" (McCracken, 1988, p. 21) when they use words that suggest a directional orientation.

▼ *Clearly mention the central concept or idea being explored or understood in the study.* Methodologically a central concept or idea is being understood, discovered, or developed in a qualitative study. This central concept may be a single idea or an umbrella idea with several sub-ideas. For example, assume that the central idea is to explore chairpersons' roles in enhancing faculty development. One might specify this central idea, as well as key terms used in this exploration, such as the roles of advocate, mentor, and coach in the study.

▼ *Provide a general definition of the central concept or idea.* Consistent with the rhetoric of qualitative research, this definition is not rigid and set, but rather is tentative and evolving throughout a study based on information from informants. Hence a writer might use the words "A tentative definition at this time for _____ is . . ." Another point: This definition is not to be confused with the detailed "definition of terms" section found later in some qualitative dissertation proposals.

The intent here is to convey to readers a general sense of the key concept so that they can better understand the study at an early juncture in the research plan.

▼ *Include words denoting the method of inquiry to be used in data collection, analysis, and the process of research* (e.g., ethnographic study, grounded-theory study, case study, a phenomenological study).

▼ *Mention the unit of analysis* (e.g., individual, group, culture) *or research site* (e.g., classroom, organization, program, event) *for the study.* A methodological characteristic of qualitative inquiry is that the study is context-bound.

Considerable variation exists in writing qualitative purpose statements, but from the above ideas, one might use a "script" to plan a purpose statement. *Scripting* is a process of completing blanks in a sentence, based on cues in the sentence. An example of a script for a qualitative purpose statement:

"The purpose of this study is (was? will be?) to _____ (understand? describe? develop? discover?) the _____ (central concept being studied) for _____ (the unit of analysis: a person? processes? groups? site?) using a _____ (method of inquiry: ethnographic design? grounded theory design? case study design? phenomenological design?) resulting in a _____ (cultural picture? grounded theory? case study? phenomenological description of themes or patterns?). At this stage in the research the _____ (central concept being studied) will be defined generally as _____ (provide a general definition of the central concept)."

The following examples may not illustrate perfectly all elements of this script, but they represent adequate models for writing qualitative purpose statements.

*Example 1. A Purpose Statement in a Phenomenology Study*

Drew (1986) conducted a phenomenologic exploration of experiences of 35 hospitalized patients in terms of the depersonalizing and confirming interactions with caregivers:

The focus of the present study was to explore distressing and nurturing encounters of patients with caregivers and to ascertain the meanings that are engendered by such encounters. The study was conducted on one of the surgical units and the obstetrical/gynecological unit of a 374-bed community hospital. (Drew, 1986, p. 40)

I found Drew's purpose statement as the first statement in a procedure discussion. She presents a single concept, "encounters," and uses good qualitative language (e.g., *explore*) and nondirectional language (both *distressing* and *nurturing*). She also mentions the site for the research.

*Example 2. A Purpose Statement in a Case Study*

Kos (1991) conducted a multiple-case study of perceptions of reading-disabled middle school students about factors that prevented these students from progressing in their reading development. Her purpose statement read:

The purpose of this study was to explore affective, social, and educational factors that may have contributed to the development of reading disabilities in four adolescents. The study also sought explanation as to why students' reading disabilities persisted despite years of instruction. This was not an intervention study and, although some students may have improved their reading, reading improvement was not the focus of the study. (Kos, 1991, pp. 876-877)

Notice Kos's disclaimer that this study was not **quantitative** by measuring the magnitude of reading changes in the students. Instead Kos clearly places this study within the qualitative approach by using such words as *explore*, focusing attention on the "factors" and providing examples of types of factors such as "affective, social, and educational."

She includes this statement under the heading "Purpose of the Study" to call attention to the statement and mentions the informants who participated in the study. One discovers, in the abstract and methodology sections of the article, that the study is a case study approach.

*Example 3.   A Purpose Statement in an Ethnographic Study*

Van Maanen (1981) discussed his role as a researcher in studying police organizations. His purpose statement was found on the third page of the study:

> The analysis that follows describes some of the situational properties, the working rules of thumb, and the social and personal identities that both characterize and define the informant game as it is played in police agencies. More broadly, this analysis represents a sort of constitutive ethnography of the fieldwork experience itself by illuminating some of the structuring activities incorporated by both the researcher and the informant as each strives to locate, understand, control, impress, deceive, predict, and otherwise come to terms with the other. The ethnographer from this standpoint is then both the researcher, and the researched. (p. 471)

This example illustrates a focus on the "informant game," and the author mentions subthemes to be explored, such as "situational properties," "working rules of thumb," and others. Moreover, the organization being studied, "police agencies," is mentioned, as is the method type of research, an ethnography.

*Example 4.   A Purpose Statement in a Grounded Theory Study*

Conrad (1978) developed a grounded theory of academic change in the curriculum through interviews on four college campuses. In the introduction to his article he presented the purpose statement:

> The primary purpose of this article is to present a grounded theory of academic change that is based upon research guided by two major research questions: What are the major sources of academic change? What are the major processes through which academic change occurs? For purposes of this paper, grounded theory is defined as theory generated from data

systematically obtained and analyzed through the constant comparative method. (Conrad, 1978, pp. 334-335)

In this statement Conrad mentions "purpose" to draw the reader's attention to the statement, states the method type of grounded theory, focuses attention on the single concept of *academic change,* and presents a definition of grounded theory for those not acquainted with qualitative designs.

## A QUANTITATIVE PURPOSE STATEMENT

**Quantitative** purpose statements differ considerably from the qualitative models just presented, in terms of the rhetorical and methodological paradigm assumptions. To properly write a quantitative statement, one needs a firm understanding of variables.

At this point it might be useful to review the meaning and use of variables. A *variable* is a discrete phenomenon that can be measured or observed in two or more categories (Kerlinger, 1979). Psychologists use the term **construct** interchangeably with **variable,** according to Kerlinger (1979). Variables could be gender, age, social economic status (SES), or attitudes or behaviors such as racism, social control, political power, and socialization. Because the phenomena vary (in two or more categories), they are called "variables." Several texts provide detailed discussions about the types of variables one can use and their scale of measurement (e.g., Isaac & Michael, 1981; Keppel, 1991; Kerlinger, 1973, 1979). In brief, variables might be distinguished by two characteristics: their temporal order and their measurement.

*Temporal order* means that one variable precedes another in time. Because of this time ordering, it is said that one variable affects or "causes" another variable (although "cause" may be questioned when dealing with human behavior) (Krathwohl, 1987; Rosenthal & Rosnow, 1991). This time ordering underlies Isaac and Michael's (1981) description of three types of variables in social science research:

Independent variables—cause, influence, or affect outcomes.

Dependent variables—are dependent on the independent variables; they are the outcomes or results of the influence of the independent variables.

Intervening (also called nuisance or extraneous or mediating) variables—intervene between the independent and dependent variables; these variables are statistically controlled in analyses. Often these variables are demographic items, such as gender, age, income, and class size.

The design of a quantitative purpose statement, therefore, begins with identifying the proposed variables for a study (independent, intervening, dependent), drawing a visual model to identify clearly this sequence, and specifying the measurement for variables. Finally the intent of using the variables quantitatively will be either to **relate** variables (as one typically finds in a survey) or to **compare** samples or groups (as is commonly found in experiments).

This knowledge helps in the design of the quantitative purpose statement. The major components of a good quantitative purpose statement consists of a brief paragraph that includes the following:

▼ *Use a word such as* **purpose, intent,** *or* **objective** *to begin the passage.* As in the **qualitative** approach, it sets the statement apart from other components of the research process. Start with "The purpose (or objective or intent) of this study is (was or will be) . . ."

▼ *Identify the theory, model, or conceptual framework to be tested in the study.* At this point one does not need to describe it in detail; in Chapter 6 I suggest a separate "theoretical perspective" section for this purpose. By mentioning the theory, one uses the deductive methodology of the **quantitative** paradigm.

▼ *Mention the specific type of method of inquiry being used in the study.* I discuss two types—the survey and the experiment—in Chapter 8.

▼ *State whether the independent and dependent variables will be related or whether two or more groups (as an independent variable) will be compared in terms of the dependent variable(s).* A characteristic of the **quantitative** methodology is that one looks for causation (cause and effect) or a relationship among variables. The words *relationship* and *comparison* are good rhetorical words denoting the cause-and-effect methodology of quantitative studies. A combination of comparing and relating might also exist—for example, a two-factor experiment wherein the researcher has two or more treatment groups, as well as a continuous variable as an independent variable in the study. Although one typically finds studies about comparing two or more groups in experiments, it is also possible to compare groups in a survey study.

▼ *As a general principle, order the variables in the relationship or comparison sentence from independent to dependent.* As mentioned earlier, in experiments the independent variable is always the "manipulated" variable.

▼ *Refer to the unit of analysis in the study.* Although **quantitative** designs are more context free than **qualitative** studies, it is useful to mention the subjects, population, or sample being studied, as well as the number of individuals studied.

▼ *Provide a general definition for each key variable in the study and use established definitions.* Another rhetorical characteristic of the **quantitative** paradigm is the use of set definitions. These definitions are meant to help the reader understand the study, and not to replace specific, operational definitions later found in a "definition of terms" section in dissertation proposals.

Based on these ideas, a quantitative purpose statement can be "scripted" to illustrate these principles. It would be as follows:

"The purpose of this _____ (experimental? survey?) study is (was? will be?) to test the theory of _____ that _____ (compares? relates?) the _____ (independent variable) to _____ (dependent variable) for _____ (subjects? sample?) at _____ (the research site). The independent variable(s) _____ will be defined generally as _____ (provide a general definition). The dependent variable(s) will be defined generally as _____ (provide a general definition), and the intervening variable(s), _____ (identify the intervening variables) will be statistically controlled in the study."

The three examples to follow illustrate many of the elements in the script. The first study was a survey; the last two were experiments.

*Example 5. A Purpose Statement in a Survey Study*

DeGraw (1984) completed a doctoral dissertation in the field of education on the topic of educators working in adult correctional institutions. Under a section titled "Statement of the Problem," he advanced the purpose of the study:

> The purpose of this study was to examine the relationship between personal characteristics and the job motivation of certified educators who taught in selected state adult correctional institutions in the United States. Personal characteristics were divided into background information about the respondent (i.e., institutional information, education level, prior training, etc.) and information about the respondents' thoughts of changing jobs. The examination of background information was important to this study because it was hoped it would be possible to identify characteristics and factors contributing to significant differences in mobility and motivation. The second part of the study asked the respondents to identify those motivational factors of concern to them. Job motivation was defined by six general factors identified in the educational work components study (EWCS) questionnaire (Miskel & Heller, 1973). These six factors are: potential for personal challenge and development; competitiveness; desirability and reward of success; tolerance for work pressures; conservative security, willingness to seek reward in spite of uncertainty vs. avoidance/ and surround concerns. (DeGraw, 1984, pp. 4-5)

This statement includes several components of a good purpose statement. It is presented in a separate section, it uses the word *relationship*, terms are defined, and the population is mentioned. Further, from the order of the variables in the statement, one can identify clearly the independent variable and the dependent variable.

*Example 6.   A Purpose Statement in an Experimental Study*

Booth-Kewley, Edwards, and Rosenfeld (1992) undertook a study comparing the social desirability of responding to a computer version of an attitude and personality questionnaire to a pencil-and-paper version. They replicated a study completed on college students that used an inventory called Balanced Inventory of Desirable Responding (BIDR), composed of two scales—impression management (IM) and self-deception (SD). In the final paragraph of the introduction, the authors advance the purpose of the study:

> We designed the present study to compare the responses of Navy recruits on the IM and SD scales, collected under three conditions—with paper-and-pencil, on a computer with backtracking allowed, and on a computer with no backtracking allowed. Approximately half of the recruits answered the questionnaire anonymously and the other half identified themselves. (Booth-Kewley et al., 1992, p. 563)

This statement also reflects many properties of a good purpose statement. The statement is separate from other ideas in the introduction (in a separate paragraph), it mentions that a comparison will be made, and it identifies the subjects in the experiment (the unit of analysis). In terms of the order of the variables, they are advanced in the statement from dependent to independent, an approach, nevertheless acceptable, that was contrary to my suggestion above. However, the issue is whether one can identify the variables, and the authors meet this criterion. Also, although the theory base is not mentioned, the paragraphs preceding the purpose statement reviewed the findings of prior theory.

## SUMMARY

In this chapter I emphasized the importance of a purpose statement in a scholarly study. This statement advances the central idea in a study; moreover, it conveys to the reader the paradigm assumptions. In writing a qualitative purpose statement, a writer needs to (a) use qualitative words that convey an evolving, developing study, (b) clearly identify the key concept being explored or understood, (c) mention the qualitative method of inquiry, (d) identify the unit of analysis, and (e) generally define terms that may not be understood by the reader. The steps are similar for a quantitative purpose statement, but writing such a statement requires a researcher to identify and understand the nature of variables and their type of measurement. Moreover, a quantitative purpose statement includes information about the theory to be used, the method of inquiry, the variables, and the intent to compare groups or samples or relate variables. It orders variables from independent to dependent in the statement, identifies the subjects or the population, and provides a general definition of variables.

## WRITING EXERCISES

1. Using the script for a qualitative purpose statement, write the statement by completing the blanks. Make this statement short; write no more than approximately three-quarters of a typed page.

2. Using the script for a quantitative purpose statement, write the statement. Also make this statement short, no longer than three-quarters of a typed page.

# ▼ ADDITIONAL READINGS

Castetter, W. B., & Heisler, R. S. (1977). **Developing and defending a dissertation proposal.** Philadelphia: University of Pennsylvania, Graduate School of Education, Center for Field Studies.

William Castetter and Richard Heisler stress the importance of the purpose or problem statement. It can take one of five forms: (a) a single question, (b) a general question followed by specific questions, (c) a general statement followed by questions, (d) a hypothesis, and (e) a general statement followed by hypotheses. Examples of each of these forms are given.

Moore, G. W. (1983). **Developing and evaluating educational research.** Boston: Little, Brown.

Gary Moore's focus is on quantitative research. He emphasizes the importance of clarity and precision in the purpose statement. Four criteria for developing and evaluating purpose statements all relate to clarity: (a) The purpose should be presented clearly and unambiguously in either declarative or question form, (b) the purpose should present the relationship between two or more variables and should state the population to be examined, (c) the variables and population specified in the purpose should be consistent with those operationalized in later sections, and (d) the purpose statement should be researchable. Each of these four criteria is discussed at length, with examples of different levels of complexity.

Wilkinson, A. M. (1991). **The scientist's handbook for writing papers and dissertations.** Englewood Cliffs, NJ: Prentice Hall.

Antoinette Wilkinson calls the purpose statement the "immediate objective" of the research study. She states that the purpose of the "objective" is to answer the research question. Further, the objective of the study needs to be presented in the introduction to a study, although it may be stated implicitly as the subject of the research, the paper, or the method. If stated explicitly, the objective is found at the end of the argument in the introduction; it also might be found near the beginning or in the middle, depending on the structure of the introduction.

# 5

▼

# *QUESTIONS, OBJECTIVES, AND HYPOTHESES*

Investigators place signposts in their research to carry the reader through a plan for a study. The first signpost was the purpose statement, which established the central direction for the study. In this chapter I address the second signpost—the research questions, objectives, or hypotheses. Questions, objectives, and hypotheses provide a specific restatement and clarification of the purpose statement. In this chapter I begin the discussion by advancing several principles involved in designing qualitative research questions and then turn to principles important for quantitative research questions, objectives, and hypotheses. These principles are discussed in view of the paradigm assumptions introduced in Chapter 1.

## QUALITATIVE RESEARCH QUESTIONS

One typically finds research questions, not objectives or hypotheses, written into qualitative studies. These research questions assume two forms: a **grand tour** question (Werner & Schoepfle, 1987) or a guiding hypothesis (Marshall & Rossman, 1989) followed by sub-**questions** (Miles & Huberman, 1984).

The *grand tour question* is a statement of the question being examined in the study in its most general form. This question, consistent with the emerging methodology of qualitative designs, is posed as a general issue so as not to limit the inquiry. One might ask, What is the broadest question that can be asked in the study? Beginning researchers trained in the **quantitative** paradigm might struggle with this approach because they are accustomed to the reverse logic: to identify specific questions or hypotheses.

▼ *I recommend that a researcher ask one or two grand tour questions followed by no more than five to seven subquestions.* This general grand tour question is followed by several subquestions that narrow the focus of the study but that do not constrain the qualitative researcher. This approach is well within the limits set by Miles and Huberman (1984), who recommend that researchers write no more than a dozen research questions in all. These questions, in turn, become topics specifically explored in interviews, observations, and documents and archival material. For example, they might be used as key questions the researcher will ask him- or herself in the observational procedure or during an open-ended interview.

▼ *The question format might be related to specific qualitative design types.* For example, the specificity of the questions in ethnography at this stage of the design differs from that in other qualitative designs. In ethnographic research, Spradley (1980) advanced a taxonomy of ethnographic questions that includes mini-tour, experience, native-language, contrast verification, rating, and 20 questions. Similarly, in critical ethnography the research questions may build on a body of existing literature. These questions become "working guidelines," rather than "truths" to be proven (Thomas, 1993, p. 35). Alternatively in phenomenology the question might be stated broadly

without specific reference to the existing literature or a typology of questions: "What is it like for a mother to live with a
teenage child who is dying of cancer?" (Nieswiadomy, 1993,
p. 151). In grounded theory the questions may be related to
procedures in the data analysis, such as open coding ("What
are the categories to emerge from interactions between caregivers and patients?") or axial coding ("How does caregiving
relate to actions by nurses?").

On the assumption that the researcher will write a grand tour
and several subquestions, the following ideas for a qualitative study
may prove helpful:

▼ *Begin the research questions with the words* what *or* how. Tell
the reader that the study will do one of the following:

discover (e.g., grounded theory)

explain or seek to understand (e.g., ethnography)

explore a process (e.g., case study)

describe the experiences (e.g., phenomenology)

These words convey the language of an emerging design of research.

▼ *Pose questions that use nondirectional wording.* These questions describe, rather than relate variables or compare groups.
Delete words that suggest or infer a **quantitative** study, words
with a directional orientation, such as *affect, influence, impact,
determine, cause,* and *relate.*

▼ *Expect the research questions to evolve and change during the
study, a thought also consistent with the assumption of an
emerging design.* Often in **qualitative** studies the questions
are under continual review and reformulation (as in a grounded
theory study). This approach may be problematic for individuals accustomed to **quantitative** designs, in which the research
questions remain fixed throughout the study.

▼ *Use open-ended questions without reference to the literature or theory unless otherwise dictated by a qualitative design type.*

▼ *Use a single focus and specify the research site in the research questions.*

The following are examples of qualitative research questions drawing on several types of designs:

*Example 1. An Ethnography*

But how are (these) conceptions of social studies played out— or not played out—in classroom practice? (**A grand tour question**) . . . How is each setting organized? (**The beginning of the subquestions**) . . . What kind of interpersonal dynamics exist? . . . How do the students, cooperating teachers, faculty members, and pupils act? . . . What activities occur in each setting? What topics are discussed, and what information, opinions, and beliefs are exchanged among the participants? (Goodman & Adler, 1985, p. 2)

*Example 2. A Grounded Theory Study*

(**Two grand tour questions are presented.**)
What are the major sources of academic change? What are the major processes through which academic change occurs? (Conrad, 1978, p. 101)

## QUANTITATIVE RESEARCH QUESTIONS, OBJECTIVES, AND HYPOTHESES

In quantitative studies, as in qualitative studies, questions, objectives, and hypotheses represent specific restatements of the purpose of the study. In survey projects these restatements typically take the form of research questions and objectives; in experiments, they are hypotheses. Especially in doctoral dissertations, advisors recommend hypotheses in experiments because they represent the traditional, classical form of raising questions.

As discussed earlier, researchers present questions, hypotheses, and objectives as either a **comparison** between two or more groups in terms of a dependent variable or as a **relationship** of two or more independent and dependent variables. Researchers also write descriptive questions to **describe** responses to the independent or dependent variables. Several general guidelines, grounded in the quantitative paradigm, might direct the development of quantitative questions, objectives, and hypotheses.

▼ *Develop the hypotheses, questions, or objectives from theory.* In the deductive methodological process of quantitative research, they are testable propositions deduced from theory (Kerlinger, 1979).

▼ *Keep the independent and dependent variables separate and measure them separately.* This procedure reinforces the cause-and-effect logic of quantitative research.

▼ *When writing this passage, select one form—write questions, objectives, or hypotheses—but not a combination.* A *hypothesis* represents a declarative statement of the relations between two or more variables (Kerlinger, 1979; Mason & Bramble, 1989). A *research question* also poses a relationship, but phrases the relationship as a question (Krathwohl, 1988); an *objective* is the same relationship statement in declarative form. Mixing hypotheses with questions or objectives conveys an informal (and redundant) style of writing.

▼ *If hypotheses are used, consider the alternative forms for writing them and make a choice based on the audience for the research.* In the rhetoric of research, the formal, traditional language is to write hypotheses. Moreover, the traditional approach is to use "null" hypotheses, which simply state that there is no significant relationship between or among the variables (e.g., There is no significant difference in the accumulation of resources and the productivity of faculty). Researchers employ this form because it has philosophical advantages in statistical testing, and good researchers tend to be conservative and cautious in their statements of conclusions (Armstrong, 1974). Alternatively one finds in current journals the use of the "directional" or "alternative" hypothesis, in which the researcher posits a direction for the relationship (e.g., The more the accumulation of resources, the more productive the researcher). One tends to use the alternative if the literature suggests a hypothesized direction for the variables (Krathwohl, 1988).

Consider, then, writing hypotheses in one of four forms: literary null, literary alternative, operational null, and operational alternative. The *literary form* means that the variables will be stated in abstract, concept-oriented language; the *operational form* represents specific language. Examples of each type of hypothesis follow.

*Example 3.  Types of Hypotheses*

**Literary null hypothesis** (concept oriented, no direction):
There is no relationship between support services and academic persistence of nontraditional-aged college women.
**Literary alternative hypothesis** (concept oriented, directional):
The more that nontraditional-aged college women use support services, the more they will persist academically.
**Operational null hypothesis** (operational, no direction):
There is no relationship between the number of hours nontraditional-aged college women use the student union and their persistence at the college after their freshman year.
**Operational alternative hypothesis** (operational, directional):
The more that nontraditional-aged college women use the student union, the more they will persist at the college after their freshman year.

*Example 4.   An Example of Literary Alternative Hypotheses*

Mascarenhas (1989) studied the differences between type of ownership (state owned, publicly traded, and private) of firms in the offshore drilling industry. Specifically the study explored such differences as domestic market dominance, international presence, and customer orientation. The study was a "controlled field study" using quasi-experimental procedures. This example illustrates hypotheses stated as "alternative" or "directional" in form, and he employed the language of variables written in the concept or "literary" form:

Hypothesis 1:Publicly traded firms will have higher growth rates than privately held firms.

Hypothesis 2:Publicly traded enterprises will have a larger international scope than state-owned and privately held firms.

Hypothesis 3:State-owned firms will have a greater share of the domestic market than publicly traded or privately held firms.

Hypothesis 4:Publicly traded firms will have broader product lines than state-owned and privately held firms.

Hypothesis 5:State-owned firms are more likely to have state-owned enterprises as customers overseas.

Hypothesis 6:State-owned firms will have a higher customer-base stability than privately held firms.

Hypothesis 7:In less visible contexts, publicly traded firms will employ more advanced technology than state-owned and privately held firms. (Mascarenhas, 1989, pp. 585-588)

▼ *Unless the study merits a close examination of demographic variables, use variables other than demographics as independent variables.* Because quantitative studies verify a theory, demographic variables (e.g., age, income level, educational level) typically enter these models as intervening or mediating variables in theories instead of major, independent variables.

▼ *Use the same pattern of word order in the questions, objectives, or hypotheses to establish a formal rhetorical style.* Repeat key phrases and order the variables by beginning with the independent and concluding with the dependent variables. An example of word order with independent variables stated first in the phrase follows.

*Example 5.  Standard Use of Language in Hypotheses*

1. **There is no relationship between** use of ancillary support services and academic persistence of nontraditional-aged college women.

2. **There is no relationship between** family support systems and academic persistence of nontraditional-aged college women.

3. **There is no relationship between** ancillary support services and family support systems.

## A MODEL FOR QUANTITATIVE
## QUESTIONS OR HYPOTHESES

▼ *Consider a model for writing questions or hypotheses based on writing descriptive questions (or hypotheses) followed by multivariate (or inferential) questions or hypotheses.* I prefer the term *multivariate* because the researcher uses multiple variables. I also employ it to reflect both independent and dependent variables, though in experimental designs, *multivariate* clearly refers only to dependent variables.

In this model the writer specifies descriptive questions for **each** independent and dependent variable (and important mediating variables) in the study. These descriptive questions then are followed by multivariate questions that relate variables or compare groups. Finally the multivariate questions are followed by questions that add any mediating or controlled variables.

*Example 6.   Descriptive and Multivariate Questions*

To illustrate this approach, assume that one wants to examine the relationship of critical thinking skills (an independent variable measured on an instrument) and student achievement (a dependent variable measured by grades) in science classes for eighth-grade students in a large metropolitan school district. One wants to control for the mediating effects (intervening variables) of prior grades in science classes and parents' educational attainment. Following the model proposed above, the research questions might be written as follows:

**Descriptive Questions**
1.  How do the students rate on critical thinking skills? (A descriptive question focused on the independent variable)
2.  What are the student's achievement levels (or grades) in science classes? (A descriptive question focused on the dependent variable)
3.  What are the student's prior grades in science classes? (A descriptive question focused on the mediating variable, prior grades)
4.  What is the educational attainment of the parents of the eighth-graders? (A descriptive question focused on the mediating variable, educational attainment of parents)

## Multivariate Questions

5. Does critical thinking ability relate to student achievement? (A multivariate question relating the independent and dependent variables)

6. Does critical thinking ability relate to student achievement, controlling for the effects of prior grades in science and the educational attainment of the eight-graders' parents? (A multivariate question relating the independent and dependent variables controlling for the mediating effects of the two intervening variables)

This example illustrates how one can take the purpose statement and first create specific research questions organized around descriptive analyses of the variables and then advance multivariate questions that relate variables. In other quantitative examples the researcher may want to compare groups, and the language may change to reflect this comparison in the multivariate questions. Still I would recommend the descriptive-multivariate model. Also, in other studies many more independent and dependent variables may be present in the model being tested, and a longer list of descriptive and multivariate questions would result.

*Example 7.   Combining Descriptive and Multivariate Questions*

In the dental school example to follow, taken from a doctoral dissertation, notice how the author writes a descriptive research question followed by a multivariate question. This study examined the relationship between organizational structure and clinical instruction in dental college clinics.

> What is the structure of clinical science instruction as measured by student/faculty ratios for each discipline in dental college clinics? . . . What are the relationships among measures of organizational size, organizational technology, organizational environment and discipline on student-faculty ratios? (DuBois, 1986, p. 13)

## SUMMARY

Research questions, objectives, and hypotheses become signposts for explaining the purpose of the study and guiding the research. Writers use all three forms in studies. Questions are the most popular form for qualitative and survey projects, and hypotheses are for experimental studies. Qualitative researchers use the model of a grand tour question followed by a small, limited number of subquestions. These questions are descriptive in nature, evolve in design, and employ appropriate qualitative language. Quantitative questions, objectives, and hypotheses flow from a theory, use a language that orders the variables from independent to dependent, often include demographic variables as mediating influences, and employ standard wording to enable a reader to understand clearly the variables in the study. A model for writing quantitative questions is to pose descriptive questions, followed by multivariate questions.

# WRITING EXERCISES

1. For a qualitative study, write one or two grand tour questions followed by five to seven subquestions.

2. For a quantitative study, write two sets of questions: In the first set pose description questions about the independent and dependent variables in the study; in the second set pose questions that relate (or compare) the independent variable(s) with the dependent variable(s).

3. Return to the working draft of your title. Retitle your study to reflect a qualitative or quantitative approach to the study. To write a qualitative title, consider the suggestions in Chapter 1 and be sure to state a central focus and use a literary style such as a question. To write a quantitative title, include the major independent and dependent variables and separate them with the conjunction *and*. Order the variables from independent to dependent so that they are consistent with the purpose statement and research questions/hypotheses.

# ▼ *ADDITIONAL READINGS*

Armstrong, R. L. (1974). Hypotheses: Why? When? How? **Phi Delta Kappan,** 54, 213-214.

In this brief article Robert Armstrong suggests that beginning researchers often are hindered by a lack of understanding of the nature and meaning of hypotheses. He provides a clear guide to the major implications of two types of hypothesis: the research hypothesis and the null hypothesis. Any hypothesis goes beyond the research question by proposing an answer. The proposed answer very likely exhibits the expectations of the researcher. However, if the research question is a genuinely exploratory one (as opposed to one seeking verification), the use of hypotheses may be inappropriate, for they will focus the researcher's efforts.

Locke, L. F., Spirduso, W. W., & Silverman, S. J. (1987). **Proposals that work: A guide for planning dissertations and grant proposals** (2nd ed.). Newbury Park, CA: Sage.

These three authors emphasize that the research question is appropriate when the research is exploratory. However, a researcher should aim to state hypotheses when existing knowledge and theory permit formulation of reasonable predictions about the relationship of variables. Hypotheses permit more powerful and persuasive conclusions than do research questions, especially if hypotheses are small and perfectly testable, rather than large and amorphous.

Marshall, C., & Rossman, G. B. (1989). **Designing qualitative research.** Newbury Park, CA: Sage.

Catherine Marshall and Gretchen Rossman emphasize how qualitative questions and problems usually come from real-world observations. These questions are not stated as hypotheses derived from theory, but rather as concerns that focus on interactions and processes in sociocultural systems and organizations. Such questions (and any subsequent answers) are enriched by the complexities of their empirical context. At the same time, Marshall and Rossman stress the need to place these research questions within a logical

framework that relates them to a tradition of inquiry and a context
of related studies.

Stock, M. (1985). **A practical guide to graduate research.** New York:
McGraw-Hill.

Molly Stock is a distinguished forestry scientist. Her book contains clear and concise advice about the design and implementation
of quantitative research projects. Emphasis is placed on the need to
develop one or more hypotheses for each question being asked in the
research and to relate each hypothesis to one or more specific
objectives. This process will ensure clarity to test each hypothesis.

# 6
▼

# *The Use of a Theory*

The hypotheses, research questions, and objectives need to be grounded in a theoretical body of knowledge in a **quantitative** study. The use of theory is introduced at this time in the design process because of its importance in explaining the hypotheses, questions, or objectives. In a quantitative dissertation an entire section of a research plan might be devoted to explicating the theory base for the study. The place of a theory (or pattern) is not as clear for a **qualitative** study. Hence this discussion is placed in the center of the book so that qualitative researchers can decide on its proper placement in their studies.

I begin the chapter by focusing on theory use in a **quantitative** study. I review a definition of a theory, the placement of it in a quantitative study, and the alternative forms it might assume in a written plan. Procedures in identifying a theory are presented next, followed by a "script" of sections to be designed in a "theoretical perspective" section of a quantitative research plan. Then I switch the discussion to use of theory in a **qualitative** study. Theories are defined as "patterns," and their use and placement in a study are noted. Finally I provide examples to illustrate the use of theories or patterns in qualitative studies.

## A QUANTITATIVE PERSPECTIVE

*Definition of a Theory*

In the **quantitative** paradigm of research, in which researchers use accepted and precise meanings, a theory commonly is understood to have certain characteristics. Kerlinger (1979) defined a theory as "a set of interrelated constructs (variables), definitions, and propositions that presents a systematic view of phenomena by specifying relations among variables, with the purpose of explaining natural phenomena" (p. 64).

Note that a *theory* is an interrelated set of constructs (or variables) formed into propositions or hypotheses that specify the relationship among variables (typically in terms of magnitude or direction). The systematic view might be an argument, a discussion, or a rationale that helps explain (or predict) phenomena that occur in the world. Labovitz and Hagedorn (1971) added to this definition the idea of a **"theoretical rationale,"** which they defined as "specifying how and why the variables and relational statements are interrelated" (p. 17). Indeed the passage that the researcher writes about the theory in a quantitative study might be called a **theory base,** a **theoretical rationale,** or a **theoretical perspective.** I prefer the term **theoretical perspective** because it is one of the headings in a proposal for a contributed paper at the American Educational Research Association.

I use the metaphor of a rainbow to explain Kerlinger's (1979) and Labovitz and Hagedorn's (1971) meaning of a theory. Assume that the rainbow **bridges** the independent and dependent variables (or constructs) in a study. This rainbow, then, ties together the variables and provides an overarching explanation for **how** and **why** one would expect the independent variable to explain or predict the dependent variable.

Independent, mediating, and dependent variables based on different forms of measures are combined into hypotheses or research questions. These hypotheses or questions provide information about the type of relationship (positive, negative, or unknown) and its magnitude (e.g., high or low). The hypothesis might be written, "The greater the centralization of power in leaders, the greater the disenfranchisement of the followers." When hypotheses such as this are tested over and over in different settings and with different populations (e.g., the Boy Scouts, a Presbyterian church, the Rotary club, a group of high school students), the statement can be elevated to the status of a theory that can be used to explain and predict disenfranchisement in organizations.

Theories vary in terms of their breadth or scope. Merriam (1988) grouped theories into three types. **Grand** theories attempt to explain large categories of phenomena and are most common in the natural sciences (e.g., Darwin's theory of evolution). **Middle-range** theories fall between minor working hypotheses of everyday life and the all-inclusive grand theories (e.g., life span development theories). **Substantive** theories are restricted to a particular setting, group, time, population, or problem (e.g., math anxiety). Any examination of the literature in the social and human sciences shows theories at all three levels. For a guide to theories and concepts useful in studying organizational topics, refer to Price and Mueller (1986). A survey of social science discipline theories can be found in Webb et al. (1986).

*Form of Theories*

The form of theories might be a series of hypotheses, "if . . . then" logic statements, or a visual model. The **form of presentation of the theory** shows a causal ordering of the variables. Hopkins (1964) presented his theory as a **series of hypotheses.** For example, Hopkins's (1964) theory of influence processes involves five variables and 15 propositions. (In the following propositions, I altered the male-specific pronouns to eliminate sex bias in the statements.) For any member of a small group:

1. The higher her rank, the greater her centrality.
2. The greater his centrality, the greater his observability.
3. The higher her rank, the greater her observability.
4. The greater his centrality, the greater his conformity.
5. The higher her rank, the greater her conformity.
6. The greater his observability, the greater his conformity.
7. The greater her conformity, the greater her observability.
8. The greater his observability, the greater his influence.
9. The greater her conformity, the greater her influence.
10. The greater his centrality, the greater his influence.
11. The greater her influence, the greater her observability.
12. The greater his influence, the greater his conformity.
13. The higher her rank, the greater her influence.
14. The greater his influence, the higher his rank.
15. The greater her centrality, the higher her rank. (p. 15)

A theory might be stated as a **series of "if . . . then" statements** that explain why one would expect the independent variables to influence or cause the dependent variables. For example, Homans (1950) explained a theory of interaction:

> If the frequency of interaction between two or more persons increases, the degree of their liking for one another will increase, and vice versa . . . persons who feel sentiments of liking for one another will express those sentiments in activities over and above the activities of the external system, and these activities may further strengthen the sentiments of liking. The more frequently persons interact with one another, the more alike in some respects both their activities and their sentiments tend to become. (pp. 112, 118, 120)

The theory may be presented as a visual model. It is useful to translate variables into a visual picture. Blalock (1969) recast verbal theories into causal models so that a reader can visualize the interconnections of independent, intervening, and dependent variables. Two simplified examples are presented here. As shown in Figure 6.1, three independent variables influence a single depend-

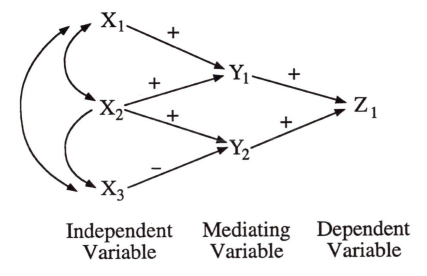

Independent     Mediating     Dependent
   Variable        Variable       Variable

**Figure 6.1.** Three Independent Variables Influence a Single Dependent Variable, Controlling for the Effects of Two Mediating Variables

ent variable mediated by the influence of two intervening variables. Duncan (1985) provided useful suggestions about the notation for constructing these visual, causal diagrams:

Position the dependent variable on the right in the diagram and the independent variables on the left.

Use one-way arrows leading from each determining variable to each variable dependent on it.

Indicate the "strength" of the relationship among variables by inserting valence signs on the paths. One may use signs (positive or negative valences) that postulate or infer relationships.

Use two-headed arrows connected by a curved line to show unanalyzed correlations between variables not dependent on others in the system.

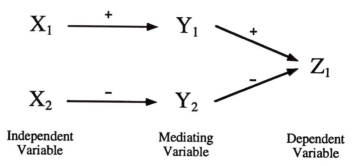

Figure 6.2. Two Groups, $X_1$ and $X_2$, Are Compared in Terms of $Z_1$, Controlling for the Effects of $Y_1$ and $Y_2$

Although more-complicated causal diagrams can be constructed with additional notation, the model presented here portrays a basic model of limited variables in a survey research study.

A variation on this theme, used in experimental studies, is to compare two groups (or samples) in terms of a dependent variable. As shown in Figure 6.2, two groups, $X_1$ and $X_2$, are compared in terms of their effect on the dependent variable, $Z_1$, controlling for the covariates $Y_1$ and $Y_2$. This design is a single factor between-subjects experimental design with covariates. The same rules of notation discussed above also apply.

The two visual models are not meant to exhaust the possibilities of connecting independent and dependent variables; more complicated designs employ multiple independent and dependent variables in elaborate models of causation (Blalock, 1969, 1985). For example, Jungnickel (1990), in a doctoral dissertation proposal, presented a complex visual model as shown in Figure 6.3.

Jungnickel asked what factors influence a faculty member's scholarly research performance. He identified these factors through a literature review and developed a model. The model follows the rules for constructing a visual model introduced earlier. The independent variables are listed on the far left, the mediating variables in the middle, and the dependent variables on the right. The direction of influence flows from left to right, and he uses + and – valences

**Independent**                                    **Dependent**

Exogenous              Endogenous

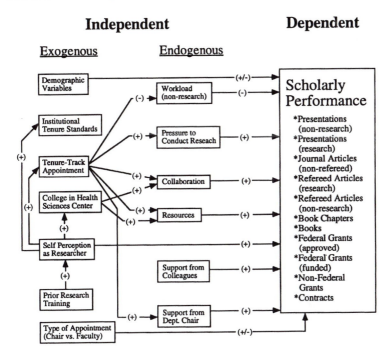

**Figure 6.3.** A Visual Model of a Theory of Faculty Scholarly Performance

SOURCE: From *Workplace Correlates and Scholarly Performance of Pharmacy Clinical Faculty Members* [Unpublished proposal] by P. W. Jungnickel, 1990, University of Nebraska, Lincoln. Used with permission.

to indicate the hypothesized direction. Overall, this theoretical framework was an adaptation of a model advanced earlier by Megel, Langston, and Creswell (1988).

*Placement of the Theory*

In **quantitative** studies one uses theory deductively and places it toward the beginning of the plan for a study. In quantitative research the objective is to test or verify a theory, rather than to develop it. One thus begins the study advancing a theory, collects data to test it, and reflects on whether the theory was confirmed or disconfirmed by the results in the study. The theory becomes a framework for the entire study, an organizing model for the

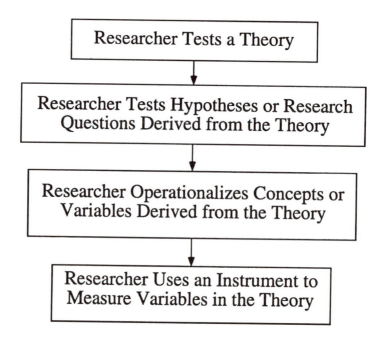

**Figure 6.4.** The Deductive Mode of Research in a Quantitative Study

research questions or hypotheses and for the data collection procedure. The deductive model of thinking used in a quantitative study is shown in Figure 6.4. The researcher tests a theory by using hypotheses or questions derived from the theory. These hypotheses or questions, in turn, contain variables that are measured by using items on an instrument.

The deductive approach to research in the quantitative paradigm has implications for the **placement of a theory** in a quantitative research study. As a general guide, the theory discussion is introduced early in a plan or study. It might be introduced in the introduction, in the literature review, immediately after hypotheses or research questions, or in a separate section of the study. Each placement has its advantages and disadvantages, as shown in Table 6.1.

My preference is to write the theory into a separate section so that readers can identify clearly the theory from other components

**Table 6.1** Options for Placing Theory in a Quantitative Study

| Placement | Advantages | Disadvantages |
| --- | --- | --- |
| In the introduction | An approach often found in journal articles, will be familiar to readers. Conveys deductive approach | It is difficult for a reader to isolate and separate theory base from other components of the research process. |
| In the literature review | Theories are found in the literature, and their inclusion in a literature review is a logical extension or part of the literature. | It is difficult for a reader to see the theory in isolation from the scholarly review of the literature. |
| After hypotheses or research questions | The theory discussion is a logical extension of hypotheses or questions because it explains how and why variables are related. | A writer may include more of a theoretical rationale after hypotheses and questions and leave out an extended discussion about the origin and use of the theory. |
| In a separate section | This approach clearly separates the theory from other components of the research process and enables a reader to better identify and understand the theory base for the study. | The theory discussion stands in isolation from other components of the research process and, as such, may not be connected easily by a reader with other components of the research process. |

of the research process. Such a separate passage provides a complete explication of the theory section, its use, and how it relates to my particular study.

## A MODEL FOR WRITING A QUANTITATIVE THEORETICAL PERSPECTIVE

Using these ideas, I would like to present a model for writing a quantitative theoretical perspective section into a research plan. Assume the task is to identify a theory that explains the relationship between **independent** and **dependent** variables. Here is a procedure that might be used:

1. Look in the discipline-based literature for a theory. If the unit of analysis for variables is individuals, look in the psychology literature; to study groups or organizations, look in the sociological literature. If the project examines individuals and groups, consider the social psychology literature. Of course, other discipline theories may be useful (e.g., to study an economic issue, the theory may be found in economics).

2. Look also at prior studies that address the topic or a closely related topic. What theories are used by other authors? Limit the number of theories; try to work with **one overarching theory** that explains the central hypothesis or research question in the study.

3. As mentioned earlier, ask the **rainbow** question: Why would the independent variable(s) influence the dependent variable(s)?

4. Script out the theory section. Follow these lead sentences:

"The theory that I will use will be _____ (name the theory). It was developed by _____ (identify the origin or source for the theory), and it was used to study _____ (identify the topics where one finds the theory being applied). This theory indicates that _____ (discuss the propositions or hypotheses in the theory). As applied to my study, this theory holds that I would expect my independent variable(s) _____ (state independent variables) to influence or explain the dependent variable(s) _____ (state dependent variables) because _____ (provide a rationale based on the logic of the theory)."

▼ *Include in a quantitative theory discussion the theory to be used, the central propositions of the theory, information about past use of the theory and its application, and statements that reflect how the theory relates to the study.*

In the example below, Crutchfield (1986) models this approach:

*Example 1.   A Quantitative Theory Section*

Crutchfield (1986) wrote a doctoral dissertation titled **Locus of Control, Interpersonal Trust, and Scholarly Productivity.** Surveying nursing educators, her intent was to determine whether locus of control and interpersonal trust affected the levels of publications of the faculty. Her dissertation included a separate section, in the

introductory chapter, called **Theoretical Perspective.** What follows
is this section; it included the following points:

---

the theory she planned to use

the central propositions of the theory

information about who has used the theory and its applicability

an adaptation of the theory to variables in her study by using the "if . . . then" logic

---

*Theoretical Perspective*

In formulation of a theoretical perspective for studying the
scholarly productivity of faculty, social learning theory provides
a useful prototype. This conception of behavior attempts
**(Author identifies the theory to be used in the study.)** to
achieve a balanced synthesis of cognitive psychology with the
principles of behavior modification (Bower & Hilgard, 1981).
Basically, this unified theoretical framework "approaches the
explanation of human behavior in terms of a continuous (reciprocal) interaction between cognitive, behavioral, and environmental determinants" (Bandura, 1977, p. vii).

While social learning theory accepts the application of reinforcements such as shaping principles, it tends to see the role
of rewards as both conveying information about the optimal
response and providing incentive motivation for a given act
because of the anticipated reward. In addition, the learning
principles of this theory place special emphasis on the important roles played by vicarious, symbolic, and self-regulating
processes (Bandura, 1971).

Social learning theory not only deals with learning, but seeks
to describe how a group of social and personal competencies
(so-called personality) could evolve out of social conditions
within which the learning occurs. It also addresses techniques
of personality assessment (Mischel, 1968), and behavior modification in clinical and educational settings (Bandura, 1977;

Bower & Hilgard, 1981; Rotter, 1954). Further, the principles of social learning theory **(Author describes social learning theory.)** have been applied to a wide range of social behavior such as competitiveness, aggressiveness, sex roles, deviance, and pathological behavior (Bandura & Walters, 1963; Bandura, 1977; Mischel, 1968; Miller & Dollard, 1941; Rotter, 1954; Staats, 1975).

**(Author describes the use of the theory.)**

Explaining social learning theory, Rotter (1954) indicated that four classes of variables must be considered: behavior, expectancies, reinforcement, and psychological situations. A general formula for behavior was proposed which states: "the potential for a behavior to occur in any specific psychological situation is the function of the expectancy that the behavior will lead to a particular reinforcement in that situation and the value of that reinforcement" (Rotter, 1975, p. 57).

*Expectancy* within the formula refers to the perceived degree of certainty (or probability) that a causal relationship generally exists between behavior and rewards. This construct of generalized expectancy has been defined as *internal* locus of control when an individual believes that reinforcements are a function of specific behavior, or as external locus of control when the effects are attributed to luck, fate, or powerful others. The perceptions of causal relationships need not be absolute positions, but rather tend to vary in degree along a continuum depending upon previous experiences and situational complexities (Rotter, 1966).

**(Author explains variables in the theory.)**

In the application of social learning theory to this study of scholarly productivity, the four classes of variables identified by Rotter (1954) will be defined in the following manner.

1. Scholarly productivity is the desired behavior or activity.

2. Locus of control is the generalized expectancy that rewards are or are not dependent upon specific behaviors.

3. Reinforcements are the rewards from scholarly work and the value attached to these rewards.

4. The educational institution is the psychological situation which furnishes many of the rewards for scholarly productivity.

With these specific variables, the formula for behavior which was developed by Rotter (1975) would be adapted to read: The potential for scholarly behavior to occur within an educational institution is a function of the expectancy that this activity will lead to specific rewards and of the value that the faculty member places on these rewards. In addition, the interaction of interpersonal trust with locus of control must be considered in relation to the expectancy of attaining rewards through behaviors as recommended in subsequent statements by Rotter (1967). Finally, certain characteristics, such as educational preparation, chronological age, post-doctoral fellowships, tenure, or full-time versus part-time employment may be associated with the scholarly productivity of nurse faculty in a manner similar to that seen within other disciplines.

**(Author applies the concepts in her study.)**

The following statement represents the underlying logic for designing and conducting this study. If faculty believe that: (a) their efforts and actions in producing scholarly works will lead to rewards (locus of control), (b) others can be relied upon to follow through on their promises (interpersonal trust), (c) the rewards for scholarly activity are worthwhile (reward values), and (d) the rewards are available within their discipline or institution (institutional setting), then they will attain high levels of scholarly productivity. (pp. 12-16; reprinted by permission of Crutchfield)

**(Author concludes with the "if . . . then" logic to relate the independent variables to the dependent variables.)**

## A QUALITATIVE PERSPECTIVE

*Theories, Patterns, and Design Types*

▼ *Use theories or patterns consistent with qualitative design type.* In qualitative research the use of theory is less clear than in quantitative designs. The term used for "theory" varies by type of design. For example, *theory* is used by those conducting grounded theory studies as an outcome for their studies. They hope to discover a theory that is grounded in information from informants. This theory would have all of the attributes (e.g., a set of interrelated constructs used to explain) mentioned in the quantitative definition provided by Kerlinger (1979). In "critical ethnographic" studies, too, researchers begin with a theory that informs their study. This causal theory might be a theory of emancipation or repression (Thomas, 1993). In ethnographic studies without a critical theory component, existing theories of culture, such as structural functionalism, symbolic interaction, social exchange theory, and others (Goetz & LeCompte, 1984), may help shape the initial research questions. In case studies, Lincoln and Guba (1985) refer to "pattern theories" as an explanation that develops during naturalistic or qualitative research. Rather than the deductive form found in quantitative studies, these pattern theories represent a "pattern" of interconnected thoughts or parts linked to a whole. Neuman (1991) provides additional information about pattern theories:

> Pattern theory does not emphasize logical deductive reasoning. Like causal theory, it contains an interconnected set of concepts and relationships, but it does not require causal statements. Instead, pattern theory uses metaphor or analogies so that relationship "makes sense." Pattern theories are systems of ideas that inform. The concepts and relations within them form a mutually reinforcing, closed system. They specify a sequence of phases or link parts to a whole. (p. 38)

Alternatively, in phenomenology no preconceived notions, expectations, or frameworks guide researchers as they analyze data (Field & Morse, 1985).

Regardless of the design type, whether theories are called "patterns," "grounded theories," or other terms (e.g., "generalizations" or "holistic pictures" as suggested by Merriam, 1988), the methodological use of some larger explanation must fit into the logic of an inductive process of research.

*Use and Placement of Theory or Pattern*

In a **qualitative** study, one does not begin with a theory to test or verify. Instead, consistent with the **inductive** model of thinking, a theory may emerge during the data collection and analysis phase of the research or be used relatively late in the research process as a basis for comparison with other theories.

▼ *View the theory or pattern as emerging in the design.* The intent is not to be constrained by a theory. Even in the most theory oriented qualitative design, such as critical ethnography, Lather (1986) qualified the use of theory:

Building empirically grounded theory requires a reciprocal relationship between data and theory. Data must be allowed to generate propositions in a dialectical manner that permits use of **a priori** theoretical frameworks, but which keeps a particular framework from becoming the container into which the data must be poured. (p. 267)

A theory may not be a "container" because it does not fit a particular situation, or it inadequately explains what is occurring naturally in a situation. One needs to build a new theory by using an inductive model of thinking or logic, as shown in Figure 6.5. The researcher begins by gathering detailed information and forms categories or themes until a theory or pattern emerges.

This inductive approach also provides a suggestion for the **placement** of theories or patterns in a qualitative study.

▼ *Place the theory or pattern late in the study and plan to contrast it with other studies.* Although the placement must be suggested by the design employed as mentioned above, the inductive process would suggest that it be used late in a study. It may be the end product of the qualitative study. For example, Lincoln and Guba (1985) discussed the intent of naturalistic studies as developing a "pattern theory." The researcher looks for categories that form a "pattern." This pattern becomes the culminating aspect of the entire study. In grounded theory Strauss and Corbin (1990) suggested that the development of a theory is the culminating aspect of a study, a theory grounded in the data. This theory might be presented as a logic diagram, a visual representation of relationships among concepts. Whether the end

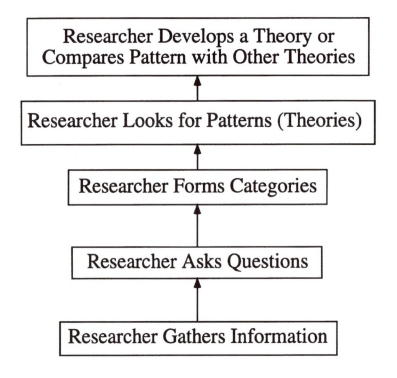

**Figure 6.5.** The Inductive Mode of Research in a Qualitative Study

product is a pattern, a generalization, or a visual model, it represents a theory developed by the researcher.

When theories are found early in studies (e.g., in the introduction), they can be viewed by a researcher as a theory in development. For example, Murguia, Padilla, and Pavel (1991) discussed Tinto's model of institutional departure in the first paragraph of their journal article. A close inspection of how they used this model reveals that they believe it had been "incompletely conceptualized and, as a consequence, only imprecisely understood and measured" (p. 433). Thus the model is not being tested in the study as one would find in a quantitative project, but rather is modified in the study.

Consistent with this line of thinking is the case in which the researcher advances a **tentative** conceptual framework in a qualitative study early in the discussion. This approach is discussed by Miles and Huberman (1984) at some length: "A conceptual framework explains, either graphically or in narrative form, the main dimensions to be studied—the key factors, or variables—and the presumed relationships among them. Frameworks come in several shapes and sizes. They can be rudimentary or elaborate, theory-driven or commonsensical, descriptive or causal" (p.28).

The evolving nature of this framework, consistent with the assumptions of an inductive qualitative design, are apparent when Miles and Huberman (1984) elaborate on how to design it:

Conceptual frameworks are best done graphically, rather than in text.

One should expect to do several iterations of these frameworks.

In multisite studies (e.g., multisite case studies), team members can create their own frameworks, and these can be compared.

Develop simplified frameworks without arrows going in all directions.

As you conduct data analysis, develop your own orienting framework and then add prior theorizing and empirical research to your framework. (p. 33)

## Examples of Theory or Pattern Use

Below I provide three illustrations of the use of theory in qualitative studies. The first, Example 2, drawn from a sociological examination of interaction of children in day care centers, illustrates a heavily oriented theoretical orientation at the beginning of the study. The second illustration, Example 3, was reported in an article in nursing wherein the author conducted a phenomenological study of nonhospitalized adults who had prior interactions with registered nurses. No theory is used or proposed in the study. The third, Example 4, is an attempt to develop a theory. This study developed a grounded theory of the role of department chairpersons in colleges and universities in enhancing the scholarly work of their faculty.

*Example 2.   Illustration of Theory Use at the Beginning of the Study*

Mandell (1984) conducted a qualitative study focusing on the interaction of children with other children in day care centers. The central concept of *role taking* by children guided the study, and the author provided an extensive discussion about the "research and theory" (p. 191) on the term *role-taking* in the opening section of the journal article. She concludes that "role-taking is then not a unitary concept. It holds a variety of meanings depending on the relationship of self-other to social objects. The more inclusive concept of negotiating meaning incorporates the varied ways in which children take account of themselves and others" (p. 193). These "variety of meanings" shape Mandell's research questions, including such questions as, "Do the children understand other's situational use of objects? Can the children act on this under-standing behaviorally (which is thus observable to a field-worker) by picking up the other's act and working that line of conduct into one's ongoing activity?" (p. 193). Following the principles of writing a theory into a qualitative study, Mandell uses the term *theory* and places the discussion toward the beginning of the study. Although the theory shaped the research questions, one does not have a sense of a theory being tested in the study.

*Example 3.   An Illustration of a Study with No A Priori Theory*

Riemen (1986) asked this question of 10 nonhospitalized adults who had prior interactions with registered nurses: "From the perspec-tive of the client, what is the essential structure of a caring nurse-client interaction?" (p. 95). A phenomenological approach was used in this descriptive study; namely, the author sought to develop a picture, rather than study cause-effect relationships. Consequently the author writes that she did not "impose an a priori hypothesis on the experience" (p. 90). The article contains no theory section, and the "picture" emerges inductively through interviews with informants. At the end of the study Riemen mentions only briefly that "the findings of this study would seem to indicate that theory development is possible concurrently with utilization of the findings" (p. 105). She ends by reviewing the key findings in the study, with no further elaboration on theory. In summary this study shows that the author (a) did not include a theory discussion (consistent with phenomenological research), (b) used the inductive approach in design, and (c) did not relate her findings to any specific theory, although she thought her findings would support theory development.

*Example 4. An Illustration of a Study That Develops Theory and Contrasts It With Other Theories*

Using a national database of 33 interviews with academic department chairpersons, Creswell and Brown (1992) developed a grounded theory interrelating variables (or categories) of chair influence on scholarly performance of faculty. The theory section comes into the article as the last section, where the authors present a visual model of the theory that was developed inductively from categories of information supplied by interviewees. In addition the authors advance directional hypotheses that logically follow from the model. Moreover, in the section on the model and the hypotheses, the authors compare their results with findings from other studies and theoretical speculations in the literature. For example, much literature exists about the career stages of faculty in academia. In terms of the proposition on the impact of career stage on the types of research issues that faculty face, the reasons for chair intervention, and the "signs" that chairs detect of problem in performance, the authors state:

> This proposition and its sub-propositions represent unusual, even contrary evidence, to our expectations. Contrary to proposition 2.1, we expected that the career stages would be similar not in type of issue but in the range of issues. Instead we found that the issues for post-tenure faculty covered almost all the possible problems on the list. Why would this group's needs be more extensive? The research productivity

literature suggests that one's research performance does not decline with the award of tenure (Holley, 1977). Perhaps diffuse career goals of post-tenure faculty expand the possibilities for "types" of issues. In any case, this subproposition focuses attention on the understudied career group that Furniss (1981) reminds us needs to be examined in more detail. (p. 58)

In summary, Creswell and Brown developed a visual model that interrelated variables, derived this model inductively from informant comments, and placed the model at the end of their study where the central propositions in it could be contrasted with the existing theories and literature.


## SUMMARY

Theory use differs between studies that use the quantitative and the qualitative paradigm of research. **Quantitative studies** employ an accepted definition of theory based on the interrelationship of variables. These variables, in turn, are related through hypotheses or research questions. When hypotheses or questions can be substantiated numerous times, they become theories that vary in their scope of application. Thus one finds grand, middle-range, and substantive theories. Researchers employ theories deductively in a quantitative study and tend to place them toward the beginning of the study. The overall model is to present a theory, gather information to test it, and return to the theory at the end of the study to determine whether it is confirmed or disconfirmed. Theories presented in the introductory passages of a study may be stated as hypotheses, if . . . then relational statements, or visual models. When writing a "theoretical perspective," consider addressing the theory to be used, the central propositions of the theory, information about past use of the theory and its application, and statements that reflect how the theory relates to the study.

Writing a theory into a **qualitative** study is more difficult because there is no standard terminology or rules about placement. The term (e.g., theory, pattern) that a researcher employs seems to vary by type of qualitative design. But all studies employ an inductive mode of development, and, therefore, the placement of theory tends to be toward the end of the study. If it is introduced at the beginning of a study, qualitative researchers modify or adjust the theory on the basis of feedback from informants in a study. Some principles to observe about using theory are as follows: (a) Employ it in a manner consistent with the type of qualitative design, (b) use it inductively so that it does not become something to test, but rather to develop and be shaped through the process of research, (c) create a visual model of the theory as it emerges, and (d) if used at the end of the study, compare and contrast it with other theories.

## WRITING EXERCISES

1. Write a "theoretical perspective" section for your research plan by following the script for a quantitative theory discussion presented in this chapter.

2. If planning a quantitative study, draw a visual model of the variables in the theory.

3. If planning a *qualitative* study, identify three or four theories that you might use to contrast with the results of your study. Describe these theories by using the *quantitative* script for a theory.

# ▼ ADDITIONAL READINGS

Blalock, H. M. (1969). **Theory construction: From verbal to mathematical formulations.** Englewood Cliffs, NJ: Prentice Hall.

> Chapter 3 of Hubert Blalock's book deals with recasting verbal theories as causal models. Blalock's ultimate goal is to provide mathematical formulations of verbal theories emanating from the social sciences. He sees the need to ensure the clarifying of concepts and the eliminating or consolidating of variables. Such a process would enable verbal theories to be seen more readily as causal models. In particular, Blalock stresses the importance of seeking relationships among independent variables so as to facilitate the building of blocks of such variables as an aid to the development of theory. He presents alternative models to visualize relationships among independent and dependent variables. He also urges that it is valuable to seek high levels of abstraction about intervening variables so as to simplify causal modeling.

Isaac, S., & Michael, W. B. (1981). **Handbook in research and evaluation: A collection of principles, methods, and strategies useful in the planning, design, and evaluation of studies in education and the behavioral sciences.** San Diego: EdITS.

> Stephen Isaac and William Michael offer a general introductory guide to the major forms of quantitative research. They provide many useful checklists to ensure compliance with generally accepted standards and practices. One such checklist identifies four major types of variables: independent, dependent, control, and intervening. The function of each type of variable is explained, as are the relationships among them.

Kerlinger, F. N. (1973). **Foundations of behavioral research.** New York: Holt, Rinehart & Winston.

> Fred Kerlinger's classic text of quantitative methodology contains a detailed discussion of types of variables. He divides them into three kinds: dependent and independent, active and attribute, and continuous and categorical. An *independent variable* is the presumed

cause of a *dependent variable*. Manipulated variables are called *active*, while measured variables are called *attributes*. *Continuous variables* are capable of taking on an ordered set of values within a certain range; *categorical variables* exist where all members of a subset are assigned the same name and the same numeral. Kerlinger also discusses intervening variables and gives numerous examples and guidance for identifying each of the types.

Krathwohl, D. R. (1987). **Social and behavioral science research: A new framework for conceptualizing, implementing, and evaluating research studies.** San Francisco: Jossey-Bass.

Chapter 9 of David Krathwohl's book deals with causal explanation of variables. In particular, it deals with the variety of issues that arise when the simple "A causes B" model seems inadequate. Krathwohl examines matters of contingency and the relationships among variables in such a way as to stress the complexities and ambiguities inherent in the notions of cause and effect.

Merriam, S. B. (1988). **Case study research in education: A qualitative approach.** San Francisco: Jossey-Bass.

Sharan Merriam emphasizes that qualitative research is more concerned with the building of theory than the testing of it. This is not to say that the researcher enters into the project with a blank mind. But it is to stress that theory must be allowed to emerge from the analysis of data. Existing theory can be used to generate new theory by linking what seems to be theoretically possible with the findings of fieldwork. Equally, theory can be generated by uncovering patterns in the data through a process such as constant comparative analysis, whereby the comparison of data leads to increasingly small numbers of conceptual categories.

Miles, M. B., & Huberman, A. M. (1984). **Qualitative data analysis: A sourcebook of new methods.** Beverly Hills, CA: Sage.

Matthew Miles and Michael Huberman discuss a rationale, a brief description, illustrations, and advice for building a qualitative conceptual framework. They suggest that all researchers, no matter how inductive in orientation, know which "bins" to start with and the general contents of bins. Laying out the bins, giving them names, and getting some clarity about their interrelationships is the rationale for a conceptual framework. This framework explains, either graphically or in narrative form, the main dimensions to be studied in a qualitative study. They can be rudimentary or elaborate, theory driven or commonsensical, descriptive or causal. Three frameworks are presented that differ in terms of their level of detail. In the advice section, Miles and Huberman suggest that the frameworks are evolving during a qualitative study.

# 7
▼

# *Definitions, Delimitations, and Significance*

In this chapter I examine aspects of a scholarly study in which the researcher bounds the study: definitions, delimitations and limitations, and the significance of the study. Boundaries are necessary in a study to provide direction for the terms used, for the scope of the study, and for the potential audience. Moreover, they represent traditional components of a scholarly study required in graduate student research. In a dissertation or a dissertation proposal, the author typically writes a separate section for each of these components; in a journal article, definitions and statements about the significance of the study are embedded within the narrative and often are described in the introduction. Delimitations and limitations are addressed in method sections. Although these components

may not be necessary in all studies, may vary in structural placement, and may not be presented within separate sections, it is important to consider essential decisions for designing them in a study.

## THE DEFINITION OF TERMS

Researchers define terms so that readers can understand the context in which the words are being used or their unusual or restricted
meaning (Castetter & Heisler, 1977). In Chapter 4 I discussed a
need for a brief definition of key variables and concepts that would
enable the reader to better understand terms in the study. Now I
focus on a detailed, more elaborate definition that will provide specific
guidance for use of terms.

*Terms to Define*

▼ *Define terms that individuals outside the field of study may not
understand.* Whether a term should be defined is a matter of
judgment; but one might define a term if there is any question
from the audience's perspective.

▼ *Define terms when they first appear so that a reader does not
read ahead in the proposal operating with one set of definitions
only to find out later that the author is using a different set.*
As Wilkinson (1991) commented: "Scientists have sharply
defined terms with which to think clearly about their research
and to communicate their findings and ideas accurately" (p. 22).
Defining terms also adds precision to a scientific study, as
Firestone (1987) stated:

The words of everyday language are rich in multiple meanings. Like other symbols, their power comes from the
combination of meaning in a specific setting. . . . Scientific
language ostensibly strips this multiplicity of meaning from
words in the interest of precision. This is the reason common terms are given "technical meanings" for scientific purposes. (p. 17)

With this need for precision, one finds terms stated early in the introduction to articles. For dissertations, terms typically are defined in a special section of the study. The rationale is that in a dissertation, students must be precise in how they use language and terms. The need to ground thoughts in authoritative definitions constitutes good science.

▼ *Define terms introduced in all sections of the research plan.* Consider terms introduced in the following sections:

the title of the study

the problem statement

the purpose statement

the research questions, hypotheses, or objectives

the literature review

the theory base of the study

the method section

## Terms in Qualitative and Quantitative Studies

Terms are defined in both **qualitative** and **quantitative** studies.

▼ **Qualitative** *studies, because of the inductive, evolving methodological design, may include few terms defined at the beginning of the plan; terms may be defined as they emerge from the data collection.* In a research plan a writer may advance "tentative" definitions because the precise definitions as used in a study will emerge from the conversations with informants in a study. Thus, for example, in an ethnographic study, themes (or perspectives or dimensions) emerge through the data analysis. An author may want to tell a reader that these themes will be defined one by one as they emerge in the study. This approach, then, to delay the definition of terms until they appear in the study, makes **a priori** definitions in qualitative studies difficult to include in research proposals. For this reason qualitative proposals often do not include separate sections on a "definition of terms," but the writer poses tentative qualitative definitions that will be used prior to entry into the field setting to gather information.

▼ *In* **quantitative** *studies, operating more within the deductive model methodology of fixed and set research objectives, one finds lengthy lists of definitions introduced early in the plan.* Moreover, they are found in a separate section in research proposals and are discussed in some detail. The researcher tries to define comprehensively all relevant terms at the beginning of a study and to use accepted definitions found in the literature.

No one approach governs how one defines the terms in a study, but several suggestions follow.

▼ *Definitions may be written at an abstract or an operational level. Operational definitions* are written in specific and detailed language; *abstract definitions,* in general language. Because the definition section in a dissertation provides an opportunity for the author to be specific about the terms being used in the study, I prefer the operational approach, especially in dissertation proposals.

▼ *In writing formal definitions in a journal article or a dissertation, use an authoritative reference (with appropriate citation) to define the term.* In this way the terms become grounded in the literature. On occasion one may not find an authoritative or accepted reference in the field for a particular term. In this case provide a definition and use it consistently throughout the plan and the study (Wilkinson, 1991).

▼ *If one writes definitions into a separate section, the "definition of terms" or "definitions" section should be written in paragraph form with the term underlined.* Typically writers do not include more than two or three pages of definitions.

The examples below illustrate acceptable formats for a dissertation proposal. The first example is a quantitative study in education, in which the researcher explored the relationship between Myers-Briggs type and leadership effectiveness of student affairs officers in colleges and universities (Wittstruck, 1986). This example illustrates the use of a separate definition section and a format for operationally defining the terms in the introduction to a study. The second example is a dissertation in sociology that examines quantitatively how divorce in the middle generation affects grandparents' relationships with their grandchildren (Vernon, 1992). Vernon includes these definitions within a section on independent variables. This example illustrates the use of more abstract definitions of terms, and terms defined without a specific reference to an authority in the literature. Notice, too, in the second example how the author relates the term to prior literature, suggesting not only the importance of the variable but also a relationship that needs to be explored.

*Example 1.  Select Terms Defined Operationally in an Education Dissertation in a Separate Section Called "Definitions"*

> *Judging* is the process of coming to conclusions about what has been perceived as measured by the Myers-Briggs Type Indicator (Myers, 1980).
>      *Leadership effectiveness,* indicated by scores on the Leadership Style Perception Instrument, is the ability of individuals to adapt their leader behaviors so that they are appropriate to the needs of the given situation (Hersey & Blanchard, 1982c). (Wittstruck, 1986, p. 7)

*Example 2.  Select Terms Abstractly Defined in an "Independent Variables" Section in a Sociology Dissertation*

> *Kinship Relationship to the Grandchild*
>
>      Kinship relationship to the grandchild refers to whether the grandparents are maternal grandparents or paternal grandparents. Previous research (e.g., Cherlin & Furstenberg, 1986) suggests that maternal grandparents tend to be closer to their grandchildren.
>
> *Sex of Grandparent*
>
>      Whether a grandparent is a grand*mother* or grand*father* has been found to be a factor in the grandparent/grandchild

relationship (i.e., grandmothers tend to be more involved than grandfathers which is thought to be related to the kinkeeping role of women within the family (e.g., Hagestad, 1988). (Vernon, 1992, pp. 35-36)

## DELIMITATIONS AND LIMITATIONS

Another parameter for a research study establishes the boundaries, exceptions, reservations, and qualifications inherent in every study: delimitations and limitations (Castetter & Heisler, 1977). It is found in both qualitative and quantitative studies.

▼ Use **delimitations** to *address how the study will be narrowed in scope.*

▼ *Provide* **limitations** *to identify potential weaknesses of the study.*

In journal articles these points are often incorporated into the method section. In proposals, either qualitative or quantitative, they are included as separate sections. Doctoral committees vary in the extent to which they require these sections. The following example, taken from a dissertation proposal in nursing (Kunes, 1991), illustrates delimitations and limitations. The first, the delimitations, suggests how the study will be narrowed in scope. The second, a limitation, indicates a potential weakness in the design of the study. Both points were included in the introduction to the proposal.

*Example 3.   A Delimitation and a Limitation*

A delimitation:

Initially, this study will confine itself to interviewing and observing the psychiatric staff nurse in a Midwest private psychiatric hospital.

A limitation:

The purposive sampling procedure decreases the generalizability of findings. This study will not be generalizable to all areas of nursing.

A limitation:

In this qualitative study, the findings could be subject to other interpretations. (Kunes, 1991, pp. 21-22)

In terms of format the delimitations and weaknesses typically are addressed in the method section in a scholarly journal article. In a dissertation they often are incorporated into a separate section titled "Delimitations and Limitations."


## SIGNIFICANCE OF THE STUDY

In dissertations a writer often includes a specific section describing the significance of the study for select audiences. In this section the writer creates a clear rationale for the importance of the study. It should expand on the "audience" point made in the introduction, in which the writer briefly mentions the problem leading to the study in light of the needs of a specific audience. Here, however, the writer can elaborate on the significance for researchers, practitioners, and policymakers. In designing this section, one might include:

three or four reasons why the study adds to the scholarly research and literature in the field

three or four reasons about how the study helps improve practice

three or four reasons why the study will improve policy

In the example to follow, the author states the significance of the study in the opening paragraphs of the journal article. This study, by Mascarenhas (1989), examined ownership of industrial firms. Decision makers, organizational members, and researchers were identified explicitly as the "audience" who would find the study useful.

*Example 4.   Significance of the Study Stated in an Introduction to a Quantitative Study*

> A study of an organization's ownership and its domain, defined here as markets served, product scope, customer orientation, and technology employed (Abell and Hammond, 1979; Abell, 1980; Perry and Rainey, 1988) is important for several reasons. First, understanding relationships among ownership and domain dimensions can help to reveal the underlying logic of organizations' activities and can help organization members evaluate strategies. . . . Second, a fundamental decision confronting all societies concerns the type of institutions to encourage or adopt for the conduct of activity. . . Knowledge of the domain consequences of different ownership types can serve as input to that decision. . . . Third, researchers have often studied organizations reflecting one or two ownership types, but their findings may have been implicitly overgeneralized to all organizations. (Mascarenhas, 1989, p. 582)

## SUMMARY

Researchers use definitions, delimitations and limitations, and statements about significance to place boundaries on their study plans. Researchers need to **define terms** that may not be understood outside the field of study; these terms should be defined at the first instance they appear in the research plan. The actual terms to be defined can be found throughout the components of a plan. In **qualitative** designs, terms are defined tentatively because the meanings of words will emerge from the informants. Also these terms are few in number and typically are defined throughout the proposed study. In **quantitative** designs, authoritative terms are defined early in the study. Researchers use separate sections to define these terms, especially in dissertation proposals. Terms may be written in more abstract language or operational language. A common approach, especially in proposals, is to write terms in paragraph form with the term underlined.

**Delimitations and limitations** address how the study will be narrowed in scope. Limitations identify potential weaknesses of a study. Their placement varies from separate sections (as in a proposal) to their incorporation into the method discussion (as in a journal article). Finally the **significance** of the study should describe the importance of the study for select audiences. Consider writing statements about the importance of the study for researchers, practitioners, and policymakers.

## WRITING EXERCISES

1. Write a definition section for your research plan. As much as possible, use authoritative references.

2. Identify how your study will be limited in scope. Write three or four reasons.

3. Identify potential limitations for your study. Focus these limitations on methodological weaknesses inherent in all study designs.

4. Write about the significance of your study. Identify how various audiences will profit from the study. Include comments about the significance for other researchers, for practitioners, and for policymakers.

# ▼ ADDITIONAL READINGS

Castetter, W. B., & Heisler, R. S. (1977). **Developing and defending a dissertation proposal.** Philadelphia: University of Pennsylvania, Graduate School of Education, Center for Field Studies.

William Castetter and Richard Heisler describe the components of a scholarly dissertation proposal. Two components to provide are definitions and a limitation section. On the one hand, the definitions not only make clear to a reader the precise language being used by the researcher but also enable a researcher to define words or phases with unusual or restricted meaning. The limitation section, on the other hand, provides a convenient place for clarifying or qualifying certain aspects of the problem addressed in the study.

Firestone, W. A. (1987). Meaning in method: The rhetoric of quantitative and qualitative research. **Educational Researcher,** 16(7), 16-21.

William Firestone discusses why terms are defined in research studies, especially in quantitative studies. He contends that the words of everyday language are rich in multiple meanings. Scientific language used in quantitative studies strips the multiplicity of meanings from words in the interest of precision. Common terms are given "technical meanings" for scientific purposes. But, he contends, a form of subterfuge exists in this process. Scientific terms must rely on their "suppressed" definitions to attract the attention of readers. For example, when behavioral psychologists refer to "learning," they make implicit reference to a wide range of situations. In this case the researcher must steer the reader's attention to specific definitions.

Wilkinson, A. M. (1991). **The scientist's handbook for writing papers and dissertations.** Englewood Cliffs, NJ: Prentice Hall.

Antoinette Wilkinson devotes an entire chapter to the use of scientific terminology. Social scientists, she suggests, must take a less-than-adequate word in our general vocabulary and define it clearly so that it delimits the exact meaning sought by the researcher. She recommends that social scientists use standard language, rather than substitute synonyms for terms. When gathering information through interview schedules, questionnaires, and analyses of texts, language becomes a direct instrument of measurement, and terms must be applied uniformly and consistently.

# 8
▼

# *A Quantitative Method*

In this chapter I present essential steps in designing a quantitative method for a research study. Specifically I advance the steps in a survey study or an experimental project. I also continue the discussion about the paradigm assumptions. For example, consistent with the methodology of a positivist framework, instruments will be used to collect data. Because reality can be measured and it exists apart from the researcher, the validity and reliability of results will become important. Through the careful design of data collection, the researcher attempts to eliminate bias and to select a representation sample from the population—all aspects of a positivist methodology. One also establishes "cause and effect" in the positivist methodology.

A caveat is in order. This discussion is not meant to be an exhaustive treatment of research methods. Excellent, detailed texts address these points (e.g., for surveys, see Babbie, 1990; Dillman, 1978; Fink & Kosecoff, 1985; Fowler, 1988; for experiments, see Keppel, 1991; Rosenthal & Rosnow, 1991). Instead I review essential components that should be discussed in a plan for research and provide a structure for writing about them.

## DEFINITIONS

A *survey* design provides a quantitative or numeric description of some fraction of the population—the sample—through the data collection process of asking questions of people (Fowler, 1988). This data collection, in turn, enables a researcher to generalize the findings from a sample of responses to a population. An *experiment* tests cause-and-effect relationships in which the researcher randomly assigns subjects to groups. The researcher manipulates one or more independent variables and determines whether these manipulations cause an outcome (McMillan & Schumacher, 1989). The researcher tests cause and effect because, theoretically, all (or most) variables between the manipulated variable and the outcome are controlled in the experiment.

## COMPONENTS OF
## A SURVEY METHOD PLAN

The design of a survey method section follows a standard format. Numerous examples of this format appear in scholarly journals, and researchers are encouraged to examine these examples for general models. Below are five typical components. Not all survey method discussions follow these five steps, but they are detailed here to illustrate a thorough plan for conducting a survey study. The following discussion reviews essential questions (as shown in Table 8.1) on a checklist that I recommend for assessing the thoroughness of a survey method plan.

**Table 8.1**    A Checklist of Questions for Designing a Survey Method

| | |
|---|---|
| _____ | Is the purpose of a survey design stated? |
| _____ | Are the reasons for choosing the design mentioned? |
| _____ | Is the nature of the survey (cross-sectional vs. longitudinal) identified? |
| _____ | Are the population and size of the population mentioned? |
| _____ | Will the population be stratified? If so, how? |
| _____ | How many people will be in the sample? On what basis was this size chosen? |
| _____ | What will be the procedure for sampling these individuals (e.g. random, nonrandom)? |
| _____ | What instrument will be used in the survey? Who developed the instrument? |
| _____ | What are the content areas addressed in the survey? The scales? |
| _____ | What procedure will be used to pilot or field test the survey? |
| _____ | What is the time line for administering the survey? |
| _____ | What are the variables in the study? |
| _____ | How do these variables cross-reference the research questions and items on the survey? |
| _____ | What specific steps will be taken in data analysis to (a) analyze returns, (b) check for response bias, (c) conduct a descriptive analysis, (d) collapse items into scales (if needed), (e) check for reliability of scales (if needed), and (f) run multivariate statistics to answer the research questions? |

*The Survey Design*

In a dissertation proposal or a journal article, the reader might be introduced to the purpose and rationale for selecting a survey design, as well as the specific type of survey design.

▼ *Begin the discussion by reviewing the purpose of a survey and the rationale for its selection as a design in the proposed study.* The topics addressed in this discussion might include the following:

Discuss the purpose of survey research. This purpose is to generalize from a sample to a population so that inferences can be made about some characteristic, attitude, or behavior of this population (Babbie, 1990). Provide a reference to this purpose from one of the survey method texts.

Indicate why a survey is the preferred type of data collection procedure for the study. Consider the advantages of survey designs, such as the economy of the design, the rapid turn-around in data collection, and the ability to identify attributes of a population from a small group of individuals as presented in Fowler (1988), Babbie (1990), Sudman and Bradburn (1986), and Fink and Kosecoff (1985).

Indicate whether the survey is cross-sectional (the survey information is collected at one point in time) or longitudinal (collected over a period of time).

Specify the form of data collection, whether it is mailed to respondents in the sample, administered in an interview format face-to-face with individuals, or gathered through telephone interviews. Provide a rationale for the data collection procedure by using arguments based on costs, availability, and convenience.

## Population and Sample

Specify the characteristics of the population and the sampling procedure. Excellent discussions have been written about the underlying logic of sampling theory (Babbie, 1990); I focus attention on essential aspects to describe in a research plan.

▼ *Describe the population in the study.* Also state the size of this population, if size can be determined, and how it will be identified. Questions of access arise here, and the researcher might refer to availability of sampling frames—mailing lists or published lists—of potential respondents in the population.

▼ *Identify whether the sampling design for this population is single stage or multistage (called clustering).* The choice may be based on access to specific individuals in a population (Babbie, 1990; Fink & Kosecoff, 1985). A single-stage sampling procedure is one in which the researcher has access to names in the population and can sample the people directly. In a multistage procedure the researcher first samples groups or organizations (or clusters), obtains names of individuals within each group or cluster, and then samples within the cluster.

▼ *Identify how individuals will be selected.* I recommend selecting a "random" sample, wherein each individual in the sample has an equal probability of being selected (a systematic sample). Less desirable is a purposive or judgmental sample, wherein potential respondents are chosen on the basis of their convenience and availability (Babbie, 1990). Undoubtedly the random procedure is most rigorous, enabling one to generalize the findings of a study to the entire population.

▼ *Discuss whether this randomly selected population will be* **stratified** *so that specific characteristics are represented in the sample and the sample reflects the true characteristics of the population* (Fowler, 1988). If one randomly selects people from a population, these characteristics may or may not be represented; stratification ensures that they will be represented.

▼ *Identify the characteristics used in stratifying the randomly selected population* (e.g., gender, income levels, education). Within each strata identify whether the sample will be chosen so that the characteristic is proportionate or disproportionate to the size of the strata (Babbie, 1990; Miller, 1991).

▼ *Indicate the procedure for selecting the random sample from lists or the sampling frame.* The most rigorous method for selecting the sample is to choose individuals randomly using a random number table located in method texts.

▼ *Indicate the number of people in the sample and how this number was determined.* I recommend that one use a sample size formula available in many survey texts (e.g., see Babbie, 1990; Fowler, 1988).

*Instrumentation*

Information about the instrument to be used in data collection is an essential component of a survey method plan. Consider the following:

▼ *Identify the survey instrument to be used in the study.* Discuss whether it is a self-designed instrument, a modified instrument, or an intact instrument developed by someone else. If a modified instrument is used, indicate whether permission has been received to use it. In some surveys the researcher constructs an instrument from components of several instruments. Permission to use parts of existing instruments needs to be obtained.

▼ *If one plans to use an existing instrument, describe the established validity and reliability of items and scales on the instrument.* This means reporting on efforts by authors to establish content validity (do the items measure the content they were intended to measure?), predictive validity (do scores predict a criterion measure?), concurrent validity (do results correlate with other results?), construct validity (do items measure hypothetical constructs or concepts?), and face validity (do the items appear to measure what the instrument purports to measure?) (Borg, Gall, & Gall, 1993). Also one might discuss reliability: measures of item consistency (are the item responses consistent across constructs?), test stability (do individuals vary in their responses when the instrument is administered a second time?), and consistency in test administration and scoring (were errors caused by carelessness in administration or scoring?) (Borg et al., 1993). When one modifies an instrument or combines instruments in a study, the original validity and reliability may be distorted, and it becomes important to reestablish validity and reliability.

▼ *Include sample items so that readers can see the actual items used.* For a journal article, one might plan to include an appendix with sample items measuring major variables in the study. For a dissertation proposal or plan, it might include attaching a complete draft of the instrument as an appendix.

▼ *Indicate the major content sections in the instrument, such as the cover letter* (Dillman, 1978, provides a useful list of items to include in cover letters), *the items* (e.g., demographics, attitudinal items, behavioral items, factual items), *and the closing instructions.* Also mention the type of scales used to measure the items on the instrument, such as rating scales (e.g., strongly agree to strongly disagree), categorical scales (e.g., yes/no), or rank-ordered scales (e.g., rank from highest to lowest importance).

▼ *Discuss plans for pilot testing or field testing the survey and provide a rationale for this procedure.* This testing is important to establish the face validity of an instrument and to improve questions, format, and the scales. Indicate the number of people with whom it will be tested and the plans to incorporate their comments into final instrument revisions.

▼ *For a mailed survey, identify steps to be taken in administering and following up the survey to obtain a high response rate.* Dillman (1978) suggested a 3-phase follow-up sequence: (a) 1 week after the original mailing, send out a postcard reminder; (b) 3 weeks later, a letter and replacement questionnaire; and (c) 7 weeks later, a letter and replacement questionnaire sent **by certified mail.** I use a 3-step procedure: (a) an initial mailing, (b) a second mailing of the complete instrument after 2 weeks, and (c) a third mailing of a postcard as a reminder to complete and send in the questionnaire. In my process this administration period covers a total of 6 weeks.

### Variables in the Study

In earlier sections of the design of a study—in the title, the purpose statement, and the research questions, hypotheses, or objectives— the reader is introduced to the variables. Now the researcher needs to relate the variables to the survey instrument. At this stage in a research plan a useful technique is to relate the variables, the research questions, and items on the survey instrument so that a reader can determine easily how questionnaire items will be used in the study.

▼ *Plan to include a table and discussion that cross-references the variables, the questions or hypotheses, and specific survey items.* This procedure is especially helpful in doctoral dissertations in which large-scale models are tested. Table 8.2 presents this form using hypothetical data.

### Data Analysis

In this section I summarize steps to be proposed in analyzing survey data.

▼ *I recommend that data analysis be presented as a series of steps* (e.g., Step 1, Step 2):

**Table 8.2**   Variables, Research Questions, and Items on Survey

| Variable Name | Research Question | Item on Survey |
|---|---|---|
| Independent Variable #1: Prior Publications | Descriptive Research Question #1: How many publications did the faculty member produce prior to receipt of the doctorate? | See Questions 11, 12, 13, 14, 15: publication counts before doctorate for journal articles, books, conference papers, book chapters |
| Dependent Variable #1: Grants Funded | Descriptive Research Question #3: How many grants has the faculty member received in the last 3 years? | See Questions 16, 17, 18: grants from foundations, federal grants, state grants |
| Mediating Variable #1: Tenure Status | Descriptive Research Question #5: Is the faculty member tenured? | See Question 19: tenured (yes/no) |

Step 1: Indicate that information will be reported about the number of returns and nonreturns of the survey. This information will be presented in table form with special attention to number of respondents and nonrespondents.

Step 2: Discuss the method by which response bias will be determined. *Response bias* is the effect of nonresponses on survey estimates (Fowler, 1988). This procedure examines whether nonrespondents had responded, whether their responses would have substantially changed the overall results of the survey.

Also provide the methods to be used. Two are popular: a wave analysis and a respondent/nonrespondent analysis. For a *wave analysis* indicate how the study will examine responses to select items (e.g., four major questions) by Week 1, Week 2, Week 3, and so forth (Leslie, 1972). Determine whether the responses change substantially from week to week. This procedure assumes that those who return surveys in the final weeks of the response period are "almost" nonrespondents. If their responses are not different from those of other weeks, a strong case for absence of response bias can be established. An alternative procedure is to contact, typically by phone, a few nonrespondents to determine whether their responses differ substantially from those of respondents. This procedure constitutes a *respondent/nonrespondent* check for response bias.

Step 3: Report that a descriptive analysis of all independent and dependent variables in the study will be conducted. This report should indicate the means, standard deviations, and range of scores for these variables. In journal articles and dissertations, descriptive statistics for survey items are found in an appendix or are summarized in the text.

Step 4: If one is building one's own scales in an instrument, discuss how survey items will be combined into scales on the independent and dependent dimensions by using factor analysis. Further report how the reliability of these scales will be checked statistically for internal consistency, a measure also demonstrating the construct validity of the scales on the instrument. One also might describe this procedure and the statistical program used.

Step 5: Identify the statistics to be used to compare groups or relate variables and answer the research questions or objectives of the study. Provide a rationale for the choice of statistics and base this rationale on (a) the unit of measurement of scales in the study, (b) the intent of the research to either relate variables or compare groups, and (c) whether the data meet the assumptions of the statistic.

## AN EXAMPLE OF
## A SURVEY METHOD

Below is an example of a survey method section that illustrates many of the steps mentioned above. This brief excerpt is taken from a journal article reporting a study of factors affecting student attrition in one small liberal arts college (Bean & Creswell, 1980, pp. 321-322).

*Methodology*

The site of this study was a small (enrollment 1,000), religious, coeducational, liberal arts college in a Midwestern city with a population of 175,000 people. The dropout rate the previous year was 25%. Dropout rates tend to be highest among freshman and sophomores, so an attempt was made to reach as many freshman and sophomores as possible by distribution of the questionnaire through classes. Research on attrition indicates that males and females drop out of college for different reasons (Bean, 1978, in press; Spady, 1971). Therefore, only women were analyzed in this study.

During April 1979, 169 women returned questionnaires. A homogeneous sample of 135 women who were 25 years old or younger, unmarried, full-time U.S. citizens, and Caucasian was selected for this analysis to exclude some possible confounding variables (Kerlinger, 1973).

**(Authors state information about the sample.)**

Of these women, 71 were freshmen, 55 were sophomores, and 9 were juniors. Of the students, 95% were between the ages of 18 and 21. This sample is biased toward higher-ability students as indicated by scores on the ACT test.

**(Authors present descriptive information about the sample.)**

Data were collected by means of a questionnaire containing 116 items. The majority of these were Likert-like items based on a scale from "a very small extent" to "a very great extent." Other questions asked for factual information, such as ACT scores, high school grades, and parents' educational level. All information used in this analysis was derived from questionnaire data. This questionnaire had been developed and tested at three other institutions before its use at this college.

**(Information is presented about the instrument.)**

Concurrent and convergent validity (Campbell & Fiske, 1959) of these measures was established through factor analysis, and was found to be at an adequate level. Reliability of the factors was established through the coefficient alpha. The constructs were represented by 25 measures—multiple items combined on the basis of factor analysis to make

indices—and 27 measures were single item indicators. Multiple regression and path analysis (Heise, 1969; Kerlinger &
Pedhazur, 1973) were used to analyze the data.

   In the causal model . . . intent to leave was regressed on
all variables which preceded it in the causal sequence. Intervening variables significantly related to intent to leave were
then regressed on organizational variables, personal variables, environmental variables, and background variables.
   (Used by permission from Bean & Creswell)
   **(Data analysis steps are presented.)**


## COMPONENTS OF
## AN EXPERIMENTAL METHOD PLAN

The components of an experimental method discussion follows
a standard form: subjects, materials, procedures, and measures.
Although these four topics are generally sufficient, in this section
I review these components, as well as several others. Thoughts
discussed here are found in standard experimental method texts
by Anderson (1971), Borg and Gall (1989), Isaac and Michael (1981),
Keppel (1991), and Rosenthal and Rosnow (1991). As with the survey
discussion, my intent is to highlight key design decisions, not to
explain the underlying theory of research methods. These key decisions can be found in a checklist of questions as shown in Table 8.3.


### Subjects

Readers need to know about the selection, assignment, and
number of subjects who will participate in the experiment. Consider the following points:

▼ *Describe whether the subjects will be selected randomly or
   conveniently.* The subjects might be selected by **random selection** or **random sampling.** The purpose of this procedure is to
   ensure that each individual has an equal probability of being
   selected from the population and that the sample will be representative of the population (Keppel, 1991). Although random

**Table 8.3**   A Checklist of Questions for Designing an Experimental
Procedure

| |
| --- |
| _____ Who are the subjects in the study? To what populations do these subjects belong? |
| _____ How were the subjects selected? Was a random selection method used? |
| _____ How will the subjects be randomly assigned? Will they be matched? How? |
| _____ How many subjects will be in the experimental and control group(s)? |
| _____ What is the dependent variable(s) in the study? How will it be measured? How many times will it be measured? |
| _____ What is the treatment condition(s)? How was it operationalized? |
| _____ Will variables be covaried in the experiment? How will they be measured? |
| _____ What experimental research design will be used? What would a visual model of this design look like? |
| _____ What instrument(s) will be used to measure the outcome in the study? Why was it chosen? Who developed it? Does it have established validity and reliability? Has permission been sought to use it? Has the author requested a fee for use of the instrument? |
| _____ What are the steps in the procedure (e.g., random assignment of subjects to groups, collection of demographic information, administration of pretest, administration of treatment(s), administration of posttest)? |
| _____ What are potential threats to internal and external validity for the experimental design and procedure? How will they be addressed? |
| _____ Will a pilot test of the experiment be conducted? |
| _____ What statistics will be used to analyze the data (e.g., descriptive and multivariate)? |

selection enables a researcher to generalize results to a population, one may need to settle for a **convenience** sample because an entire group of individuals (e.g., a classroom, an organization, a family unit) is available to participate in the study. Alternatively a **convenience** sample may consist of volunteers who enlist to participate in the study.

▼ *Indicate whether the subjects will be assigned randomly to groups in the experiment.* In many experiments, in addition to random selection, investigators use **random assignment,** whereby the subjects are assigned randomly to groups or treatment conditions. This procedure eliminates the possibility of systematic differences occurring among subjects and the environment of the experiment that could affect outcomes (Keppel, 1991). To illustrate this procedure, the researcher might randomly assign volunteer subjects to two treatment groups so that an equal number of subjects participates in each treatment.

▼ *Indicate whether the subjects will be matched, as well as randomly assigned to treatment groups.* Matching subjects is used if the subjects in the conditions will be comparable on a pretest that measures the dependent variables or on variables highly correlated with the dependent variable (Borg & Gall, 1989). The criteria for matching might be ability levels or demographic variables. A researcher may decide not to match, however, because it is expensive, takes time (Salkind, 1990), and leads to incomparable groups if subjects leave the experiment (Rosenthal & Rosnow, 1991).

▼ *Tell the reader about the number of subjects in each group and the procedure for determining the size of each group.* It is important to ground the determination of **size** in a systematic procedure. Overall, researchers design experiments that are sensitive to the possibility of significant treatment effects through choosing rigorous levels of significance, selecting sensitive designs such as repeated measures and stratification, and controlling for variables through covariance (Keppel, 1991). In addition one can choose an appropriate size of treatment group to increase the power of the study. This selection can be accomplished through the use of power tables, which provide the number of subjects for each group in the experiment, given the effects of power or sensitivity of the experiment, the effect size, and the significance level (Cohen, 1977; Keppel, 1991). Experiments should be planned so that the size of each treatment group provides the greatest sensitivity that the effect on the outcome is actually due to the experimental manipulation in the study.

### The Variables

▼ *Identify the* **independent variables,** *called* **treatment conditions** *or* **factors** *in an experiment.* These treatment conditions are under the control of the researcher and typically are manipulated in an experiment. As independent variables they "lead to" changes in the dependent variable.

No single, agreed-on classification of independent variables exists, but Rosenthal and Rosnow (1991) suggested five examples: biological events (e.g., food deprivation), social environment (e.g., sociocultural pressures and demographics), hereditary factors (e.g., health problems), previous training and experience, and maturity (e.g., age of subjects, level of social maturity). In some cases the independent variables represent the manipulation (e.g, an experimenter assesses the effects of a teaching method, randomly assigning subjects to the experimental and control groups). In other cases the independent variables are treatments given to preassigned groups that may vary on ability level or demographic characteristics (Campbell & Stanley, 1966). In this latter category the researcher is not strictly manipulating the independent variable because factors such as ability level and demographic characteristics cannot be altered.

▼ *Identify the* **dependent variable** *or variables to be used in the study.* The dependent variable is the response or the **criterion** variable presumed to be "caused" or influenced by the independent treatment conditions. As with the independent variables, no set classification system exists. But Rosenthal and Rosnow (1991) advanced three prototypic outcome measures in experiments: the direction of observed change, the amount of this change, and the ease with which the change is effected (e.g., subject reacquires the correct response as in a single-subject design). The investigator needs to specify which outcome or outcomes are being studied.

### Instrumentation and Materials

During an experiment one makes observations or obtains measures by using instruments at a pretest or posttest (or both) stage of design. As with the selection of all instruments, a sound research plan calls for a thorough discussion about the instrument or instruments—their development, items, scales, and reliability and validity. Also the researcher will use materials in the experiment for the treatment conditions that likewise need to be explained.

▼ *Describe the instrument or instruments to be used in the experiment.* Indicate whether they have established validity and reliability (by using criteria mentioned earlier for survey instruments: content validity, predictive validity; concurrent validity; construct validity; and face validity [Borg et al.,

1993]), who developed them, and the permission sought to use them.

▼ *Discuss thoroughly the materials used to create the treatment conditions.* One group, for example, may participate in a special computer-assisted learning plan used by a teacher in the classroom. This plan will involve handouts, lessons, and special written instructions to help students in this experimental group learn how to study a subject by using computers. A pilot test of these materials may be discussed. The intent of this test is to administer materials without variability to the experimental groups.

*The Experimental Design*

The design of an experiment involves using a type of experimental procedure. One needs to indicate the overall type, the independent variables, and a clear visual model for the procedure.

▼ *Discuss the overall type of design.* The types available in experiments are preexperimental, quasi-experimental, single-subject, and the pure experiment. With **preexperimental** designs, the research does not have a control group to compare with the experimental group. In **quasi-experimental** designs, control and experimental groups are used in the study, but subjects are not randomly assigned to the groups. A **single-subject** design or *N* of 1 design involves observing the behavior of a single individual (or individuals) over time. In a **pure experiment** the subjects are assigned randomly to the treatment groups.

▼ *Other distinctions can be made about the overall experimental design in terms of the specific use of independent variables.* Many experiments involve **between-subject** designs, wherein different individuals are assigned to treatment groups (Keppel, 1991; Rosenthal & Rosnow, 1991). More complex experimental studies may use subjects in more than one treatment or multiple independent conditions. In this **within-subject** design (or **repeated measures** design), the same set of subjects participating in the experiment is assigned to different treatments. This design raises questions, however, about the **order**

**effects,** wherein the order of treatment effects in the administration of the experiment may influence outcomes because subjects become sensitized to treatments. Steps are available to correct this problem (Borg & Gall, 1989).

**Factorial designs** are employed when researchers cross the levels of one treatment with all of the levels of another (Campbell & Stanley, 1966; Cook & Campbell, 1979). These designs assess the main effects of each treatment, as well as the interaction effects of different treatments. A widely used behavioral research design, this design explores not only the effects of each treatment separately but also in combination, thereby providing a rich and revealing multidimensional view (Keppel, 1991).

▼ *Provide a diagram or a figure to illustrate the specific research design to be used.* A standard notation systems needs to be used in this figure. I recommend that one use a classic—the notations provided by Campbell and Stanley (1966). This notation is as follows:

X represents an exposure of a group to an experimental variable or event, the effects of which are to be measured.

O represents an observation or measurement.

X's and O's in a given row are applied to the same specific persons. X's and O's vertical to one another are simultaneous.

The left-to-right dimension indicates the temporal order (sometimes indicated with an arrow).

The symbol R indicates random assignment.

Parallel rows separated by a dashed line mean comparison groups not equated by random assignment. (p. 6)

This notation is used in illustrations of experimental designs.

*Example 1. Preexperimental Designs*

**One-Shot Case Study:** This design involves an exposure of a group to a treatment followed by a measure.

Group A   X——-O

**One Group Pretest-Posttest Design:** This design includes a pretest measure followed by a treatment and a posttest for a single group.

Group A      O1 ——— X ——— O2

**Static Group Comparison or Posttest Only With Nonequivalent Groups:** This design frequently is used after a treatment has been implemented. After the treatment, the researcher selects a comparison group and applies a posttest to both the experimental and comparison groups.

Group A     X ——— O
            ―――
Group B          O

**Alternative Treatment Posttest-Only With Nonequivalent Groups Design:** This design uses the same procedure as the above static group comparison, with the exception that the nonequivalent comparison group received a different treatment.

Group A     X1 ——— O
            ―――
Group B     X2 ——— O

*Example 2.Quasi-Experimental Designs*

**Nonequivalent (Pretest and Posttest) Control Group Design:** In this design, a popular approach to quasi-experiments, the experimental Group A and the control Group B are selected without random assignment. Both groups take a pretest and a posttest, and only the experimental group received the treatment.

Group A     O —— X —— O

Group B     O ——————— O

**Single-Group Interrupted Time-Series Design:** In this design the researcher records measures for a single group and observes their behavior both before and after a treatment.

Group A     O—O—O—O—X—O—O—O—O—O

**Control Group Interrupted Time-Series Design:** A modification of the single group interrupted design wherein two groups of subjects, not randomly assigned, are observed over time. A treatment is administered to only one of the groups (Group A).

Group A     O—O—O—O—X—O—O—O—O—O

Group B     O—O—O—O—O—O—O—O—O—O

*Example 3. True Experimental Designs*

**Pretest-Posttest Control Group Design:** A traditional, classic design, this procedure involves the random assignment of subjects to two groups, the administration of a pretest and a posttest to both groups, and the treatment administered to only the experimental Group A.

Group A     R——-O——-X——-O
Group B     R—— O——————— O

**Posttest-Only Control Group Design:** This design controls for any confounding effects of a pretest and is a popular experimental design. The subjects are assigned randomly to groups, a pretest and the treatment are given to only the experimental group, and both groups are measured on the posttest.

Group A     R —— O —— X —— O
Group B     R ——————————— O

**Solomon Four Group Design:** A special case of a $2 \times 2$ factorial design, this procedure involves the random assignment of subjects to four groups. Pretests and treatments are varied for the four groups. All groups receive a posttest.

```
Group A    R —— O —— X —— O
Group B    R —— O ————————— O
Group C    R—— X —— O
Group D    R ————————— O
```

*Example 4.  Single Subject*

**A-B-A Single-Subject Design:** This design involves multiple observations of a single individual. The target behavior of a single individual is established over time—called the baseline. Once stability of this baseline is established, the researcher administers a treatment. Observations continue over time after the treatment has been removed.

```
Baseline A          Treatment B              Baseline A
                   X—X—X—X—X—X
O—O—O—O—O—O—O—O—O—O—O—O—O—O—O—O
```

▼ *Identify threats to the internal and external validity of the experiment and relate these threats to the type of design proposed for the study.* According to Isaac and Michael (1981), **internal validity** addresses whether the experimental manipulation in a specific study really will make a difference. **External validity** assesses whether the findings will be representative and whether the results can be generalized to similar circumstances and subjects.

Refer to a table in a methods text that identifies the threats (e.g., Borg & Gall, 1989; McMillan & Schumacher, 1989). Since Campbell and Stanley (1966) first mentioned this subject, the list of potential threats has grown. For example, Borg and Gall (1989) mentioned 12 types of threats to internal validity and 2 threats to external validity. The choice of any experimental design is to minimize the threats to internal validity and to balance factors that can be control-led in an experiment with the realities of real-life experimental situations.

## The Procedure

One needs to describe in detail the procedure for conducting the experiment. A reader should be able to see the design being used, the observations, the treatment, and the time line of activities.

▼ *Discuss a step-by-step approach for the procedure in the experiment.* For example, Borg and Gall (1989) outlined six steps typically used in the procedure for a pretest-posttest control group design with matching:

1. Administer to the research subjects measures of the dependent variable or a variable closely correlated with the dependent variable.
2. Assign subjects to matched pairs on the basis of their scores on the measures described in Step 1.
3. Randomly assign one member of each pair to the experimental group and the other member to the control group.
4. Expose the experimental group to the experimental treatment and administer no treatment or an alternative treatment to the control group.
5. Administer measures of the dependent variables to the experimental and control groups.
6. Compare the performance of the experimental and control group on the posttest(s) by using tests of statistical significance. (p. 679)

## Statistical Analysis

Tell the reader about the types of statistical analysis that will be used during the experiment.

▼ *Describe the descriptive statistics calculated for observations and measures at the pretest or posttest stages of experimental designs.* These statistics are means, standard deviations, and ranges.

▼ *Describe the inferential statistics used to test the hypotheses in the study.* For experimental designs with categorical information (groups) on the independent variable and continuous information on the dependent variable, $t$ tests or univariate analysis of variance (ANOVA), analysis of covariance (ANCOVA), or multivariate analysis of variance (MANOVA— multiple dependent measures) often are used to determine the statistical significance of mean score differences among treatment groups. In factorial designs, one looks for both main and interaction effects. Nonparametric statistical equivalents are used when the scores on a pretest or posttest show marked deviation from a normal distribution.

▼ *For single-subject research designs, use line graphs for baseline and treatment observations for abscissa (horizontal line) units of time and the ordinate (vertical line) target behavior.* Each data point is plotted separately on the graph, and the data points are connected by lines. Occasionally tests of statistical significance, such as $t$ tests, are used to compare the pooled mean of the baseline and the treatment phases, although such procedures may violate the assumption of independent measures (Borg & Gall, 1989).

## AN EXAMPLE OF
## AN EXPERIMENTAL METHOD SECTION

The following is a selected passage from a quasi-experimental study by Enns and Hackett (1990) that demonstrates many of the components in an experimental design. Their study addressed the general issue of matching client and counselor interests along the dimensions of attitudes toward feminism. They hypothesized that feminist subjects would be more receptive to a radical feminist counselor whereas nonfeminist subjects would rate the nonsexist and liberal feminist counselor more positively. Except for a discussion about data analysis, their approach in the method discussion seems consistent with the parts mentioned above.

*Method*

*Subjects*

The subjects were 150 undergraduate women enrolled in both lower- and upper-division courses in sociology, psychology, and communications at a midsized university and a community college, both on the West Coast. . . .

**(The authors describe the subjects participating in this study.)**

*Design and Experimental Manipulation*

This study used a 3 × 2 × 2 factorial design: Orientation of Counselor (nonsexist-humanistic, liberal feminist, or radical feminist) × Statement of Values (implicit or explicit) × Subjects' Identification with Feminism (feminist or nonfeminist). Occasional missing data on particular items were handled by a pairwise deletion procedure.

**(Authors describe the overall design.)**

The three counseling conditions, nonsexist-humanistic, liberal, and radical feminist, were depicted by 10 min. videotape vignettes of a second counseling session between a female counselor and a female client. . . . The implicit statement of values condition used the sample interview only; the counselor's values were therefore implicit in her responses. The explicit statement of values condition was created by adding to each of the three counseling conditions a 2-min. leader that portrayed the counselor describing to the client her counseling approach and associated values including for the two feminist conditions a description of her feminist philosophical orientation, liberal or radical. . . . Three counseling scripts were initially developed on the basis of distinctions between nonsexist-humanistic, liberal, and radical feminist philosophies and attendant counseling implications. Client statements and the outcome of each interview were held constant, whereas counselor responses differed by approach.

**(Authors describe the three independent variables manipulated in the study.)**

*Instruments*

**Manipulation checks.** As a check on subjects' perception
of the experimental manipulation and as an assessment of
subjects' perceived similarity to the three counselors, two
subscales of Berryman-Fink and Verderber's (1985) Attribu-
tions of the Term Feminist Scale were revised and used in
this study as the Counselor Description Questionnaire
(CDQ) and the Personal Description Questionnaire (PDQ).
. . . Berryman-Fink and Verderber (1985) reported internal
consistency reliabilities of .86 and .89 for the original ver-
sions of these two subscales . . . Attitudes Toward Feminism
Scale (AFT) . . . Counselor Rating Form-Short (CRF S) . . .
Counselor Preference Questionnaire (CPQ) . . . Perceptions
of the Counselor Scale . . . Open-ended question.
     **(Authors discuss the instruments and the reliability of
the scales for the dependent variable in the study.)**

*Procedure*

     All experimental sessions were conducted individually.
The experimenter, an advanced doctoral student in counseling psychology, greeted each subject, explained the purpose
of the study as assessing students' reactions to counseling,
and administered the ATF. The ATF was then collected and
scored while each subject completed a demographic data
form and reviewed a set of instructions for viewing the videotape. The first half of the sample was randomly assigned to
one of the twelve videotapes (3 Approaches × 2 Statements
× 2 Counselors), and a median was obtained on the ATF.
The median for the first half of the sample was then used
to categorize the second half of the group as feminist or
nonfeminist, and the remainder of the subjects were randomly assigned to conditions separately from each feminist
orientation group to ensure nearly equal cell sizes. The median on the final sample was checked and a few subjects re-
categorized by the final median split, which resulted in 12
or 13 subjects per cell.
     After viewing the videotape that corresponded to their ex-
perimental assignment, subjects completed the dependent
measures and were debriefed. (pp. 35-36. Copyright 1990 by

the American Psychological Association. Reprinted by permission.)
**(Authors describe the procedure used in the experiment.)**

## SUMMARY

In this chapter I identified essential components in designing a method procedure for a survey or experimental study. The steps for a survey study began with a discussion about the purpose of a survey design; the identification of the population and sample for the study; the survey instruments to be used; the relationship between the variables, the research questions, specific items on the survey; and steps to be taken in the analysis of data from the survey. In the design of an experiment, the researcher mentions subjects participating in the study; the variables—the treatment conditions and the criterion variables; the instruments used for pretests and posttests and the materials to be used in the treatments; the specific type of experimental design—whether it is a preexperimental, quasi-experimental, single-subject, or pure experiment and a illustration of the design; threats to internal and external validity that relate to the design of choice; and the statistical analysis used to test the hypotheses.

# WRITING EXERCISES

1. Design a plan for the procedures to be used in a survey study. Review the checklist in Table 8.1 after you write the section to determine whether all components have been addressed.

2. Design a plan for procedures for an experimental study. Refer to Table 8.3 after you complete your plan to determine whether all questions have been addressed adequately.

# ▼ ADDITIONAL READINGS

Babbie, E. (1990). **Survey research methods** (2nd ed.). Belmont, CA: Wadsworth.

Earl Babbie provides a thorough, detailed text about all aspects of survey design. He reviews the types of study designs and the logic of sampling, provides examples of designs, and discusses the conceptualization of a survey instrument and its scales. He then provides useful ideas about administering a questionnaire and processing the results. Also included is a discussion about data analysis, with attention to constructing and understanding tables and writing a survey report. This book is detailed, informative, and technically oriented toward students at the intermediate or advanced level of survey research.

Borg, W. R., & Gall, M. D. (1989). **Educational research: An introduction** (5th ed.). New York: Longman.

Walter Borg and Meredith Gall discuss experimental designs in educational research in two sections. They cover much of the same ground offered in other experimental method texts—types of designs, validity issues, and statistical techniques. Specific examples provide useful material to understand the topics. Their discussion about validity issues is especially strong and comprehensive. Factorial designs are explained in detail with good illustrations.

Campbell, D. T., & Stanley, J. C. (1966). Experimental and quasi-experimental designs for research. In N. L. Gage (Ed.), **Handbook of research on teaching** (pp. 1-76). Chicago: Rand McNally.

This chapter in the Gage **Handbook** is the classical statement about experimental designs. Donald Campbell and Julian Stanley design a notation system for experiments that is used today; they also advance the types of experimental designs, beginning with factors that jeopardize internal and external validity, the preexperimental design types, true experiments, quasi-experimental designs, and correlational and ex post facto designs. The authors present an excellent summary of types of designs, threats to validity, and statistical procedures to test the designs. This is an essential chapter for students beginning their study of experimental studies.

Fink, A., & Kosecoff, J. (1985). **How to conduct surveys: A step-by-step guide.** Newbury Park, CA: Sage.

In a text filled with many examples, Arlene Fink and Jacqueline Kosecoff discuss basic survey construction issues such as designing a questionnaire using good questions, appropriate format and length, adequate sample size and response rate, types of survey designs, analyzing survey information, and presenting survey results in summaries, pictures, and graphs.

Fowler, F. J. (1988). **Survey research methods.** Newbury Park, CA: Sage.

Floyd Fowler provides a useful text about the decisions that go into the design of a survey research project. He addresses using alternative sampling procedures, reducing nonresponse rates, collecting data, designing good questions, employing sound interviewing techniques, preparing surveys for analysis, and addressing ethical issues in survey designs.

Isaac, S., & Michael, W. B. (1981). **Handbook in research and evaluation: A collection of principles, methods, and strategies useful in the planning, design, and evaluation of studies in education and the behavioral sciences** (2nd ed.). San Diego: EdITS.

In Chapter 2 of this book Stephen Isaac and William Michael provide a guide to the types of research designs available in the behavioral sciences, including the quasi- and true experimental designs. In sections on experimental designs, they provide statements about the purpose, examples, the characteristics, and the essential steps involved in using the designs. For example, the seven steps in experimental research closely follow the steps in an experimental design mentioned in the present chapter. As in most method texts, Isaac and Michael also provide an overview about validity. The discussions about design procedures for each type of experimental design give detailed examples for researchers to follow. An additional section in this chapter highlights some "concerns, strategies, and pitfalls" in the design of research. This section is important reading because of the concluding section on such topics as control of large samples versus small samples, matching, making meaningful comparisons, and other topics that undergird experimental research designs.

Keppel, G. (1991). **Design and analysis: A researcher's handbook** (3rd ed.). Englewood Cliffs, NJ: Prentice Hall.

Geoffrey Keppel provides a detailed, thorough treatment of the design of experiments from the principles of design to the statistical analysis of experimental data. Overall this book is for the mid-level to advanced statistics student who seeks to understand the design and statistical analysis of experiments. The introductory chapter advances an informative overview of the components of experimental designs.

McMillan, J. H., & Schumacher, S. (1989). **Research in education: A conceptual introduction.** New York: HarperCollins.

In Chapter 9 of this introductory text, James McMillan and Sally Schumacher provide an overview of experimental, single-subject, and ex post facto designs. Each type of design is reviewed, and the reader is introduced to a visual model of the design and a detailed description of the threats to validity for the particular design. As an introduction to experimental research, this text is excellent for the beginner.

Rosenthal, R., & Rosnow, R. L. (1991). **Essentials of behavioral research: Methods and data analysis (2nd ed.).** New York: McGraw-Hill.

Robert Rosenthal and Ralph Rosnow cover topics about types of experimental designs, threats to validity, and advances topics about the selection of subjects and stimuli. In addition, they devote an entire chapter to discussing the structure and logic of experimental designs in which one reviews basic considerations such as randomization, independent and dependent variables, and the concept of causality, factors important in understanding the underlying assumptions of experimental research.

# 9
## ▼

# *A Qualitative Procedure*

Unlike with quantitative designs, few writers agree on a precise procedure for data collection, analysis, and reporting of qualitative research. Unfortunately, reading qualitative journal articles provides little assistance because authors truncate the steps in order to emphasize results or to meet editorial restrictions on length. Limited discussion, however, is available in Marshall and Rossman (1989) and Wolcott (1990). In this chapter I rely on their suggestions, employ examples from journals and dissertations, and incorporate my own experiences. As in the prior chapter, this discussion does not address details about procedures; instead the focus is on key design decisions for planning a study.

The procedure for a qualitative study includes advancing the assumptions of qualitative designs, indicating the specific type of

**Table 9.1**    A Checklist of Questions for Designing a Qualitative Procedure

_____    Are the basic characteristics or assumptions of qualitative studies
          mentioned?
_____    Does the reader gain an understanding of the differences between
          qualitative and quantitative approaches?
_____    Is the specific type of qualitative design to be used in the study
          mentioned? Is enough background about this design mentioned so that
          the reader understands the discipline origin of the design, a definition
          for the design, and any special characteristics of the design?
_____    Does the reader gain an understanding of the experiences of the
          researcher that shape his or her values and biases brought to the
          research?
_____    Is a description provided about the steps taken to gain entry and
          approval to collect data at the research site?
_____    Are the procedures for collecting data mentioned and discussed? Are
          the reasons for using the data collection procedures mentioned?
_____    Are the procedures for recording information during the data collection
          procedure mentioned?
_____    Are the data analysis steps of coding the information mentioned?
_____    Are the data analysis steps of analyzing the information by using
          specific data analysis procedures advanced in specific designs (e.g.,
          ethnographic approaches, grounded theory, case study, phenomenology)
          mentioned?
_____    Are the steps to be taken to verify the information (validity and
          reliability) mentioned? Does one gain an understanding of the limita-
          tions of qualitative designs in terms of generalizing and replicating
          the findings?
_____    Is a specific outcome for the study (e.g., a case study, a grounded theory)
          mentioned? Is this outcome discussed in light of existing theory and
          literature?

design, reflecting on the researcher's role, discussing data collection, developing data recording procedures, identifying data analysis procedures, specifying verification steps, and delineating the narrative outcomes of the study. After discussing each of these steps in detail, I end the chapter with an example that illustrates many of the steps in a qualitative procedure section. A checklist provided in Table 9.1 indicates questions one might ask at each step in the procedure.

## THE ASSUMPTIONS
## OF QUALITATIVE DESIGNS

In Chapter 1 I reviewed the assumptions of the qualitative paradigm of research. As one plans his or her procedure, it might prove useful to review these assumptions. For audiences familiar with qualitative research, this section may not be needed.

▼ *Discuss four or five underlying assumptions or basic characteristics of the qualitative mode of inquiry and refer to distinctions between* **qualitative** *and* **quantitative** *research.* Two approaches may be used, depending on the philosophical sophistication of the audience. One approach is to refer to the qualitative paradigm assumptions and differences in Table 1.1 and provide specific examples to illustrate the qualitative paradigm assumptions. A second approach is to rely on the assumptions primarily about the methodology of the research as advanced in several introductory qualitative research texts (e.g., Bogdan & Biklen, 1992; Eisner, 1991; Merriam, 1988) or journal articles (e.g., Firestone, 1987). For example, Merriam (1988) mentioned six assumptions:

1. Qualitative researchers are concerned primarily with **process,** rather than outcomes or products.
2. Qualitative researchers are interested in **meaning**—how people make sense of their lives, experiences, and their structures of the world.
3. The qualitative researcher is the **primary instrument** for data collection and analysis. Data are mediated through this human instrument, rather than through inventories, questionnaires, or machines.
4. Qualitative research involves **fieldwork.** The researcher physically goes to the people, setting, site, or institution to observe or record behavior in its natural setting.
5. Qualitative research is **descriptive** in that the researcher is interested in process, meaning, and understanding gained through words or pictures.
6. The process of qualitative research is **inductive** in that the researcher builds abstractions, concepts, hypotheses, and theories from details. (pp. 19-20)

▼ *Discuss why the problem is well suited to a qualitative design.*
In Table 1.2 I suggested that qualitative research is exploratory
and that researchers use it to explore a topic when the variables
and theory base are unknown. In addition I find Morse (1991)
helpful. She states:

Characteristics of a qualitative research problem are: (a) the
concept is "immature" due to a conspicuous lack of theory and
previous research; (b) a notion that the available theory may
be inaccurate, inappropriate, incorrect, or biased; (c) a need
exists to explore and describe the phenomena and to develop
theory; or (d) the nature of the phenomenon may not be
suited to quantitative measures. (p. 120)

## THE TYPE OF DESIGN

▼ *Indicate the specific qualitative design—the approach to data
collection, analysis, and report writing—to be used.* This passage
is important because of the growing awareness among qualitative researchers about alternative designs and their distinctive
characteristics. Tesch (1990), for example, advanced a typology of
20 design types organized into those that explore the **characteristics of language, discover regularities,** seek **a comprehension
of the meaning of text/action,** and advance **reflection.** These
types have their origin in sociology, psychology, and education.
Educator M. Smith (1987) categorized qualitative approaches into
**interpretive, artistic, systematic,** and **theory-driven approaches.**
From a broader social science perspective, Jacob (1987) compared and described the "traditions" of qualitative research as
**ecological psychology, holistic ethnography, cognitive anthro-
pology, ethnography of communication,** and **symbolic interactionism.** Lancy (1993) reviewed qualitative approaches in
anthropology, sociology, human ethnology, ecological psychology, cognitive studies, and history.

Those who conduct qualitative research, then, are faced with many
possibilities of design drawn from disciplinary fields of anthropol-

ogy, psychology, social psychology, sociology, and education. In this book I have emphasized approaches drawn from sociology (grounded theory), anthropology (ethnography), psychology (phenomenology), and political science and many social sciences (case studies).

▼ *Describe characteristics of the design.* For example, the plan might address

---

the discipline field where the design originated

a good definition for the design

the typical unit of analysis used in the design

alternative types of problems often studied by using the design

various data collection processes

different data analysis processes

typical formats for reporting the information

any other special characteristic of the design

---

## THE RESEARCHER'S ROLE

Qualitative research is interpretative research. As such, the biases, values, and judgment of the researcher become stated explicitly in the research report. Such openness is considered to be useful and positive (Locke, Spirduso, & Silverman, 1987). Gaining entry to a research site and the ethical issues that might arise are two elements of this role.

▼ *Include statements about past experiences of the researcher that provide familiarity with the topic, the setting, or the informants.* These experiences likely will shape the interpretation of the report.

▼ *Discuss steps taken to gain entry to the setting and to secure permission to study the informants or situation* (Marshall &

Rossman, 1989). It is important to gain access to research or archival sites by seeking the approval of "gatekeepers." Gaining entry may be a continuous problem in a research project when the researcher moves from one site to another (Marshall & Rossman, 1989). Perhaps a brief proposal needs to be developed and submitted for the review by gatekeepers. Bogdan and Biklen (1992) advanced topics that could be addressed in such a proposal:

Why was the site chosen for study?

What will be done at the site during the research study?

Will it be disruptive?

How will the results be reported?

What will the "gatekeeper" gain from the study?

▼ *Indicate steps taken to obtain permission from the Institutional Review Board (if needed) so that the rights of human subjects are protected.*

▼ *Comment about sensitive ethical issues such as maintaining confidentiality of data, preserving the anonymity of informants, and using research for intended purposes* (Merriam, 1988).

## THE DATA COLLECTION PROCEDURES

The data collection steps involve (a) setting the boundaries for the study, (b) collecting information through observations, interviews, documents, and visual materials, and (c) establishing the protocol for recording information.

▼ *Identify the parameters for the data collection.* The idea of qualitative research is to **purposefully** select informants (or documents or visual material) that will best answer the research question. No attempt is made to randomly select informants. Beyond

**Table 9.2**   A Compendium of Data Collection Approaches in Qualitative Research

---

- Gather observational notes by conducting an observation as a participant.
- Gather observational notes by conducting an observation as an observer.
- Conduct an unstructured, open-ended interview and take interview notes.
- Conduct an unstructured, open-ended interview, audiotape the interview, and transcribe the interview.
- Keep a journal during the research study.
- Have an informant keep a journal during the research study.
- Collect personal letters from informants.
- Analyze public documents (e.g., official memos, minutes, archival material).
- Examine autobiographies and biographies.
- Examine physical trace evidence (e.g., footprints in the snow).
- Videotape a social situation or an individual/group.
- Examine photographs or videotapes.
- Have informants take photographs or videotapes.
- Collect sounds (e.g., musical sounds, a child's laughter, car horns honking).

---

this general parameter, researchers should consider four parameters suggested by Miles and Huberman (1984): the **setting** (where the research will take place); the **actors** (who will be observed or interviewed); the **events** (what the actors will be observed doing or interviewed about); and the **process** (the evolving nature of events undertaken by the actors within the setting).

▼ *Indicate the type or types of data to be collected and provide a rationale for the data collection.* Data collection procedures in qualitative research involve four basic types: observations, interviews, documents, and visual images. A compendium of data collection approaches drawing on all four types is presented in Table 9.2. As shown in Table 9.3, each type has advantages and limitations. In many qualitative studies, multiple data collection procedures are used.

## DATA RECORDING PROCEDURES

Before entering the field, qualitative researchers plan their approach to data recording. What is to be recorded? and How will it be recorded? are two critical concerns to be addressed.

**Table 9.3** Qualitative Data Collection Types, Options, Advantages, and Limitations

| Data Collection Types | Options Within Types | Advantages of the Type | Limitations of the Type |
|---|---|---|---|
| Observations | Complete participant —researcher conceals role<br>Observer as participant —role of researcher is known<br>Participant as observer—observation role secondary to participant role<br>Complete observer—researcher observes without participating | Researcher has firsthand experience with informant.<br>Researcher can record information as it occurs.<br>Unusual aspects can be noticed during observation.<br>Useful in exploring topics that may be uncomfortable for informants to discuss. | Researcher may be seen as intrusive.<br>"Private" information may be observed that researcher cannot report.<br>Researcher may not have good attending and observing skills.<br>Certain informants (e.g., children) may present special problems in gaining rapport. |
| Interviews | Face-to-face—one on one, in-person interview<br>Telephone—researcher interviews by phone<br>Group—researcher interviews informants in a group | Useful when informants cannot be directly observed.<br>Informants can provide historical information.<br>Allows researcher "control" over the line of questioning. | Provides "indirect" information filtered through the views of interviewees.<br>Provides information in a designated "place," rather than the natural field setting.<br>Researcher's presence may bias responses.<br>Not all people are equally articulate and perceptive. |
| Documents | Public documents such as minutes of meetings, newspapers<br>Private documents such as journal | Enables a researcher to obtain the language and words of informants.<br>Can be accessed at a time con- | May be protected information unavailable to public or private access. |

| | | venient to researcher—an unobtrusive source of information. | Requires the researcher to search out the information in hard-to-find places. |
|---|---|---|---|
| | or diary, letter | Represents data that are thoughtful in that informants have given attention to compiling. As written evidence, it saves a researcher the time and expense of transcribing. | Requires transcribing or optically scanning for computer entry. Materials may be incomplete. The documents may not be authentic or accurate. |
| Audiovisual Materials | Photographs Videotapes Art objects Computer software Film | May be an unobtrusive method of collecting data. Provides an opportunity for informant to share directly his or her "reality." Creative in that it captures attention visually. | May be difficult to interpret. May not be accessible publicly or privately. The presence of an observer (e.g., photographer) may be disruptive and affect responses. |

NOTE: This table includes material taken from Merriam (1988) and Bogdan & Biklen (1992).

▼ *Design and advance protocols for collecting information.* Researchers engage in multiple **observations** during the course of a qualitative study. A **protocol** or form for recording information is needed to note observations in the field. One might design an observational protocol as a single page with a dividing line down the middle to separate **descriptive notes**—portraits of the informants, a reconstruction of dialogue, a description of the physical setting, accounts of particular events, and activities—from **reflective notes**—an opportunity for the researcher to record personal thoughts such as "speculation, feelings, problems, ideas, hunches, impressions, and prejudices" (Bogdan & Biklen, 1992, p. 121). Also on this form, one might include **demographic information** about the time, place, and date that describe the field setting where the observation takes place.

A protocol is also useful in conducting **interviews.** This protocol would include the following components: (a) a heading, (b) instructions to the interviewer (opening statements), (c) the key research questions to be asked, (d) probes to follow key questions, (e) transition messages for the interviewer, (f) space for recording the interviewer's comments, and (g) space in which the researcher records reflective notes. If information is to be quantified, each question needs to be referenced to a column number for recording the numbers when information is transferred from the interviews to a computer format.

Researchers record information from interviews by using note taking or audiotapes. I recommend that one audiotape each interview and then transcribe the interview later. Also during the interview, the researcher should take notes in the event that the recording equipment fails. Planning in advance for the needs of a transcriptionist is important.

The recording of **documents and visual materials** can follow the protocol format outlined above. A protocol for recording information could be established that identifies (a) information about the document or material and (b) key categories that the researcher is looking for in the source of information. With documents, it would be helpful to note whether the information represents primary material (information directly from the people or situation being studied) or secondary material (secondhand accounts of the people or situation).

## DATA ANALYSIS PROCEDURES

Several components might comprise the discussion about the plan for analyzing the data. The process of data analysis is **eclectic;** there is no "right way" (Tesch, 1990). Metaphors and analogies are as appropriate as open-ended questions. Data analysis requires that the researcher be comfortable with developing categories and making comparisons and contrasts. It also requires that the researcher be open to possibilities and see contrary or alternative explanations for the findings. Also the tendency is for beginning researchers to collect much more information than they can manage or reduce to a meaningful analysis. As Patton (1980) noted:

> The data generated by qualitative methods are voluminous. I have found no way of preparing students for the sheer massive volumes of information with which they will find themselves confronted when data collection has ended. Sitting down to make sense out of pages of interviews and whole files of field notes can be overwhelming. (p. 297)

These caveats aside, several points can guide the development of the analysis of qualitative data.

▼ *Suggest in the plan that the data analysis will be conducted as an activity* **simultaneously** *with data collection, data interpretation, and narrative reporting writing.* In this respect **qualitative** analysis clearly differs from the **quantitative** approach of dividing and engaging in the separate activities of data collection, analysis, and writing the results. In **qualitative** analysis several simultaneous activities engage the attention of the researcher: collecting information from the field, sorting the information into categories, formatting the information into a story or picture, and actually writing the qualitative text. These activities, especially for an experienced researcher, proceed simultaneously, though beginning researchers may want to treat them separately (Bogdan & Biklen, 1992).

▼ *Indicate how the process of qualitative analysis will be based on data* **"reduction"** *and* **"interpretation"** (Marshall & Rossman, 1989, p. 114). The researcher takes a voluminous amount of information and reduces it to certain patterns, categories, or themes and then interprets this information by using some schema. Tesch (1990) called this process "de-contextualization" and "re-contextualization." This process results in a "higher level" analysis: "While much work in the analysis process consists of 'taking apart' (for instance, into smaller pieces), the final goal is the emergence of a larger, consolidated picture" (Tesch, 1990, p. 97).

▼ *Mention a plan for representing the information in matrices.* Miles and Huberman (1984) support the concept of *displays* of the information, a spatial format that presents information systematically to the reader. These displays are tables of tabular information. They show the relationship among categories of information, display categories by informants, site, demographic variables, time ordering of the information, role ordering, and many other possibilities.

▼ *Identify the coding procedure to be used to reduce the information to themes or categories.* Flexible rules govern how one goes about sorting through interview transcriptions, observational notes, documents, and visual material. It is clear, however, that one forms categories of information and attaches codes to these categories. These categories and codes form the basis for the emerging story to be told by the qualitative researcher. This process involves what has been called "segmenting" the information (Tesch, 1990), developing "coding categories" (Bogdan & Biklen, 1992), and "generating categories, themes, or patterns" (Marshall & Rossman, 1989). Assume that one is working with interview transcriptions of *unstructured data*, data that have been collected through interview questions with little structure to shape the responses from the informant. Tesch (1990) provided eight steps to consider:

1. Get a sense of the whole. Read through all of the transcriptions carefully. Perhaps jot down some ideas as they come to mind.

2. Pick one document (one interview)—the most interesting, the shortest, the one on the top of the pile. Go through it, asking yourself, What is this about? Do not think about the "substance" of the information, but rather its underlying meaning. Write thoughts in the margin.

3. When you have completed this task for several informants, make a list of all topics. Cluster together similar topics. Form these topics into columns that might be arrayed as major topics, unique topics, and leftovers.

4. Now take this list and go back to your data. Abbreviate the topics as codes and write the codes next to the appropriate segments of the text. Try out this preliminary organizing scheme to see whether new categories and codes emerge.

5. Find the most descriptive wording for your topics and turn them into categories. Look for reducing your total list of categories by grouping topics that relate to each other. Perhaps draw lines between your categories to show interrelationships.

6. Make a final decision on the abbreviation for each category and alphabetize these codes.

7. Assemble the data material belonging to each category in one place and perform a preliminary analysis.

8. If necessary, recode your existing data. (pp. 142-145)

These eight steps engage a researcher in a systematic process of analyzing textual data. Certainly variations exist in this process. For example, some researchers have found it useful to color code different categories on transcripts. Also look for unusual or useful quotes that later will be incorporated into the qualitative story. Researchers, too, may want to develop their lists of categories that reflect major and minor themes in the data. One list could be designated specifically as information that demonstrates information "contrary" to the emerging themes. The process of sorting information might be done with file folders, file cards, or computer software (Merriam, 1988). One might consider coding categories as topical areas themselves, as suggested by Bogdan and Biklen (1992). These authors suggested that one can use setting and context codes

perspectives held by subjects

subjects' ways of thinking about people and objects

process codes

activity codes

strategy codes

relationship and social structure codes

preassigned coding schemes (pp. 167-172)

In addition to discussing the coding procedure, tell the reader about the use of computer software, if used, to analyze the data. Tesch (1990) reviewed the qualitative text software packages available for MS-DOS and Macintosh computers. These software programs work on the principle of allowing the researcher to identify text segments, attach category labels to the segments, and sort for all text segments that relate to a specific category. When one reviews hundreds of pages of transcriptions or field notes, these computer programs can provide a more efficient system for retrieving and sorting information than the traditional card-sort method.

▼ *Mention any specific data analysis procedures that are inherent in qualitative designs.* Some design types in qualitative research have detailed protocols for data analysis. For example, Strauss and Corbin (1990) provided a series of data analysis steps for **grounded theory** that consists of open coding, axial coding, selective coding, and the generation of a conditional matrix. The researcher in this process attempts to saturate categories through "constantly comparing" incidents with incidents until categories emerge and through the sampling of informants (theoretical sampling) that will lead to the development of categories. In **case study** research Yin (1989) discussed dominant modes of data analysis, such as (a) the search for "patterns" by comparing results with patterns predicted from theory or the literature; (b) "explanation building," in which the researcher looks for causal links and/or explores plausible or rival explanations and attempts to build an explanation about the case; and (c) "time-series analysis," in which the researcher traces changes in a pattern over time, a procedure similar to time-series analysis conducted in experiments and quasi-experiments.

In **ethnographic research** Spradley (1980) suggested procedures such as (a) "domain analysis," the search for a semantic relationship in the data (e.g., "X is a kind of Y" and developing a worksheet that displays these relationships); (b) developing a "taxonomy" wherein the researcher displays the relationship among all of the included terms in the domain in a branch diagram, a content outline, or tabular forms; (c) a "componential analysis," which shows differences among informants on select criteria; and (d) a "thematic" analysis that encompasses the earlier three types. In **phenomenology,** although the steps for data analysis are less structured and more open to alternative procedures, Dukes (1984) suggested that one look for "structural invariants" of a particular type of experience—the patterns—and then submit these patterns to a different researcher for confirmation.

## VERIFICATION STEPS

Determining the accuracy of the account, discussing the generalizability of it, and advancing possibilities of replicating a study have long been considered the scientific evidence of a scholarly study. Qualitative researchers have no single stance or consensus on addressing traditional topics such as validity and reliability in qualitative studies. Early qualitative researchers felt compelled to relate traditional notions of validity and reliability to the procedures in qualitative research (e.g., see Goetz & LeCompte, 1984). Later qualitative writers developed their own language to distance themselves from the positivist paradigms. Lincoln and Guba (1985) and, more recently, Erlandson, Harris, Skipper, and Allen (1993) discuss establishing quality criteria such as "trustworthiness" and "authenticity." These are all viable stances on the question of validity and reliability.

My perspective is to suggest the importance of addressing the concepts of *validity* and *reliability* in a qualitative plan and to frame these concepts within the procedures that have emerged from qualitative writings. My stance is allied with comments by Merriam (1988) and Miles and Huberman (1984).

▼ Describe how the study will address the issue of **internal validity,** *the accuracy of the information and whether it matches reality* (Merriam, 1988). Several procedures might be discussed in specific reference to the study (Merriam, 1988; Miles & Huberman, 1984) that lend internal validity to a study:

---

Discuss plans to triangulate, or find convergence among sources of information, different investigators, or different methods of data collection. For example, another researcher might provide an "audit" trail of the key decisions made during the research process and validate that they were good decisions.

Discuss plans to receive feedback from informants (also called "member checks"). Take the categories or themes back to the informants and ask whether the conclusions are accurate.

Identify how informants and participants will be involved in all phases of the research. The epistemological assumption of the qualitative paradigm is based on minimizing the distance between the researcher and the informant (Guba & Lincoln, 1988). Thus key informants might be identified for interviews or observation, participants might be data gatherers, and they might review the findings as they emerge.

---

▼ Discuss the limited generalizability of findings from the study— the **external validity.** As mentioned by Merriam (1988), the intent of qualitative research is not to generalize findings, but to form a unique interpretation of events. This point aside, however, limited generalizability might be discussed for the categories or themes to emerge from the data analysis or for the data collection protocol used by the researcher.

▼ *Discuss limitations in replicating the study—the* **reliability** issue. Like the issue of generalizability, the uniqueness of a study within a specific context mitigates against replicating it exactly in another context. However, statements about the researcher's positions—the central assumptions, the selection of informants, the biases and values of the researcher—enhance the study's chances of being replicated in another setting. In case study research, in which the investigator explores multisite cases, one can examine whether the same patterns or events or thematic constructs are replicated in different settings. In fact, Yin (1989) strongly suggested reporting a detailed protocol for data collection so that the procedure of a qualitative case study might be replicated in another setting.

## THE QUALITATIVE NARRATIVE

A plan for a qualitative procedure should end with some comments about the narrative that emerges from the data analysis. Qualitative research narratives present information in text or image forms (e.g., photographs, videotapes). The variety of narratives that exist is extensive, and examples from scholarly journals will illustrate models. In a plan for a study, consider advancing several points about the narrative:

▼ *Indicate the forms to be used in the narrative.* At the macro level one finds possibilities such as the types of narrative tales: the *realist tale,* a direct, matter-of-fact portrait without information about how the field-worker produced the portrait; the *confessional tale,* with a focus on the field-worker, rather than on the subjects being studied; and the *impressionist tale,* "fleeting moments of fieldwork cast in dramatic form" (Van Maanen,

1988, p. 7). At the micro level one might include discussion of the narrative conventions such as:

varying the use of long, short, and text-embedded quotes

scripting conversation

presenting text information in tabular form (e.g., matrices)

using category names from the informants

intertwining quotations with (author's) interpretations

using indents to signify informant quotes

using the first person *I* or collective *we* in the narrative form

using metaphors (e.g., see Richardson, 1990, who discusses some of these forms)

▼ *Relate how the narrative outcome will be related to design types.* For **case studies** consider a single case or multicase or cross-case comparison; a holistic (single unit of analysis) or an embedded analysis (multiple units of analysis); or one of Yin's (1989) illustrative structures—linear-analytic, comparative, chronological, theory building, suspense, or unsequenced. For **ethnographies** consider establishing dimensions or perspectives; using Spradley's (1980) six levels of writing an ethnography (universal statements, cross-cultural descriptions, general statements about society, specific context, specific statements about culture, actual behaviors); or tell a story. For **grounded theory** (Strauss & Corbin, 1990) consider presenting information from open coding—a list of categories or taxonomy; using axial coding and drawing a visual that explains propositions or hypotheses; or developing a story that relates the open and axial coding to one category (selective coding). For **phenomenology** the outcome typically consists of a descriptive narrative, a synthesis of knowledge about the phenomenon under study. For example, Riemen (1986), in a nursing study of "caring," reported clusters of themes that were common from and common to all of the subject's descriptions. Then she reported an "exhaustive description" of a caring interaction between a nurse and a client.

▼ *Describe how the narrative outcome will be compared to theories and the general literature on the topic.* In many qualitative articles, one finds the literature discussed in the final section, after the author has reported the narrative outcome in the study. In an inductive, emerging design, the literature and theory as discussed in Chapters 2 and 6 can be used as a basis of comparison for the cultural portrait, the case study, the grounded theory, or the narrative description. Typically this comparison is made in narrative form, but a table comparing and contrasting themes is a useful alternative.


## AN EXAMPLE

The following is an example of a qualitative procedure written as part of a dissertation proposal (Miller, 1992). Miller's project was an ethnographic study of first-year experiences of a 4-year college president. As I present this discussion, I will refer back to the sections addressed in this chapter.

*The Qualitative Research Paradigm*

The qualitative research paradigm has its roots in cultural anthropology and American sociology (Kirk & Miller, 1986). It has only recently been adopted by educational researchers (Borg & Gall, 1989). The intent of qualitative research is to understand a particular social situation, event, role, group, or interaction (Locke, Spirduso, & Silverman, 1987). It is largely an investigative process where the researcher gradually makes sense of a social phenomenon by contrasting, comparing, replicating, cataloguing and classifying the object of study (Miles & Huberman, 1984). Marshall and Rossman (1989) suggest that this entails immersion in the everyday life of the setting chosen for the study; the researcher enters the informants world and through ongoing interaction, seeks the informants' perspectives and meanings.

**(Qualitative assumptions are mentioned.)**

Scholars contend that qualitative research can be distinguished from quantitative methodology by numerous unique characteristics that are inherent in the design. The following is a synthesis of commonly articulated assumptions regarding characteristics presented by various researchers.

1. Qualitative research occurs in natural settings, where human behavior and events occur.

2. Qualitative research is based on assumptions that are very different from quantitative designs. Theory or hypotheses are not established **a priori.**

3. The researcher is the primary instrument in data collection rather than some inanimate mechanism (Eisner, 1991; Fraenkel & Wallen, 1990; Lincoln & Guba, 1985; Merriam, 1988).

4. The data that emerge from a qualitative study are descriptive. That is, data are reported in words (primarily the participant's words) or pictures, rather than in numbers (Fraenkel & Wallen, 1990; Locke et al., 1987; Marshall & Rossman, 1989; Merriam, 1988).

5. The focus of qualitative research is on participants' perceptions and experiences, and the way they make sense of their lives (Fraenkel & Wallen, 1990; Locke et al., 1987; Merriam, 1988). The attempt is therefore to understand not one, but multiple realities (Lincoln & Guba, 1985).

6. Qualitative research focuses on the process that is occurring as well as the product or outcome. Researchers are particularly interested in understanding how things occur (Fraenkel & Wallen, 1990; Merriam, 1988).

7. Idiographic interpretation is utilized. In other words, attention is paid to particulars; and data are interpreted in regard to the particulars of a case rather than generalizations.

8. Qualitative research is an emergent design in its negotiated outcomes. Meanings and interpretations are negotiated with human data sources because it is the subjects' realities that the researcher attempts to reconstruct (Lincoln & Guba, 1985; Merriam, 1988).

9. This research tradition relies on the utilization of tacit knowledge (intuitive and felt knowledge) because often the nuances of the multiple realities can be appreciated most in this way (Lincoln & Guba, 1985). Therefore, data are not quantifiable in the traditional sense of the word.

10. Objectivity and truthfulness are critical to both research traditions. However, the criteria for judging a qualitative study differ from quantitative research. First and foremost, the researcher seeks believability, based on coherence, insight and instrumental utility (Eisner, 1991) and trustworthiness (Lincoln & Guba, 1985) through a process of verification rather than through traditional validity and reliability measures.

### The Ethnographic Research Design

This study will utilize the ethnographic research tradition. This design emerged from the field of anthropology, primarily from the contributions of Bronislaw Malinowski, Robert Park and Franz Boas (Jacob, 1987; Kirk & Miller, 1986). The intent of ethnographic research is to obtain a holistic picture of the subject of study with emphasis on portraying the everyday experiences of individuals by observing and interviewing them and relevant others (Fraenkel & Wallen, 1990). The ethnographic study includes in-depth interviewing and continual and ongoing participant observation of a situation (Jacob, 1987) and in attempting to capture the whole picture reveals how people describe and structure their world (Fraenkel & Wallen, 1990).

**(The author uses the ethnographic approach.)**

### The Researcher's Role

Particularly in qualitative research the role of the researcher as the primary data collection instrument necessitates the identification of personal values, assumptions and biases at the outset of the study. The investigator's contribution to the research setting can be useful and positive rather than detrimental (Locke et al., 1987). My perceptions of higher education and the college presidency have been shaped by my personal experiences. From August 1980 to May 1990 I served as a college administrator on private campuses of 600 to 5,000. Most recently (1987-1990) I was Dean for Student Life at a small college in the Midwest. As a member of the President's cabinet, I was involved with all top level administrative cabinet activities and decisions and worked closely with the faculty, cabinet officers, president and board of trustees. In addition to reporting to the president, I worked with him through his

first year in office. I believe this understanding of the context
and role enhances my awareness, knowledge and sensitivity
to many of the challenges, decisions and issues encountered
as a first year president and will assist me in working with the
informant in this study. I bring knowledge of both the structure of higher education and the role of the college presidency.
Particular attention will be paid to the role of the new president
in initiating change, relationship building, decision making,
and providing leadership and vision.

Due to previous experiences working closely with a new college president, I bring certain biases to this study. Although
every effort will be made to ensure objectivity, these biases
may shape the way I view and understand the data I collect
and the way I interpret my experiences. I commence this study
with the perspective that the college presidency is a diverse
and often difficult position. Though expectations are immense,
I question how much power the president has to initiate
change and provide leadership and vision. I view the first year
as critical; filled with adjustments, frustrations, unantici-
pated surprises and challenges.

**(Researcher's biases are stated.)**

*Bounding the Study and Data Collection*

*Setting*

This study will be conducted on the campus of a state college
in the Midwest. The college is situated in a rural Midwestern
community. The institution's 1,700 students nearly triple the
town's population of 1,000 when classes are in session. The institution awards associate, bachelor and master's degrees in 51
majors.

*Actors*

The informant in this study is the new President of a state
college in the Midwest. The primary informant in this study
is the President. However, I will be observing him in the
context of administrative cabinet meetings. The president's
cabinet includes three Vice Presidents (Academic Affairs,

Administration, Student Affairs) and two Deans (Graduate Studies and Continuing Education).

## Events

Using ethnographic research methodology, the focus of this study will be the everyday experiences and events of the new college president, and the perceptions and meaning attached to those experiences as expressed by the informant. This includes the assimilation of surprising events or information, and making sense of critical events and issues that arise.

## Processes

Particular attention will be paid to the role of the new president in initiating change, relationship building, decision making, and providing leadership and vision.
**(Parameters of the study are mentioned.)**

## Ethical Considerations

Most authors who discuss qualitative research design address the importance of ethical considerations (Locke et al., 1982; Marshall & Rossman, 1989; Merriam, 1988; Spradley, 1980). First and foremost, the researcher has an obligation to respect the rights, needs, values, and desires of the informant(s). To an extent, ethnographic research is always obtrusive. Participant observation invades the life of the informant (Spradley, 1980) and sensitive information is frequently revealed. This is of particular concern in this study where the informant's position and institution are highly visible. The following safeguards will be employed to protect the informant's rights: 1) the research objectives will be articulated verbally and in writing so that they are clearly understood by the informant (including a description of how data will be used), 2) written permission to proceed with the study as articulated will be received from the informant, 3) a research exemption form will be filed with the Institutional Review Board (Appendix B1 and B2), 4) the informant will be informed of all data collection devices and activities, 5) verbatim transcriptions and written interpretations and reports will be made available to the informant, 6) the informant's rights, interests and wishes will be considered first when choices are made regarding reporting the data, and 7) the final decision regarding informant anonymity will rest with the informant.

**(How author addresses ethical issues and IRB review.)**

*Data Collection Strategies*

Data will be collected from February through May 1992. This will include a minimum of bi-monthly, 45 minute recorded interviews with the informant (initial interview questions, Appendix C), bi-monthly two hour observations of administrative cabinet meetings, bi-monthly two hour observations of daily activities and bi-monthly analysis of the president's calendar and documents (meeting minutes, memos, publications). In addition, the informant has agreed to record impressions of his experiences, thoughts and feelings in a taped diary (guidelines for recorded reflection, Appendix D). Two follow-up interviews will be scheduled for the end of May 1992 (See Appendix E for proposed timeline and activity schedule).

**(The author plans to use face-to-face interviews, participate as observer, and obtain private documents.)**

To assist in the data collection phase I will utilize a field log, providing a detailed account of ways I plan to spend my time when I am on-site, and in the transcription and analysis phase (also comparing this record to how time is actually spent). I intend to record details related to my observations in a field notebook and keep a field diary to chronicle my own thinking, feeling, experiences and perceptions throughout the research process.

**(The author records descriptive and reflective information.)**

*Data Analysis Procedures*

Merriam (1988) and Marshall and Rossman (1989) contend that data collection and data analysis must be a simultaneous process in qualitative research. Schatzman and Strauss (1973) claim that qualitative data analysis primarily entails classifying things, persons, and events and the properties which characterize them. Typically throughout the data analysis process ethnographers index or code their data using as many categories as possible (Jacob, 1987). They seek to identify and describe patterns and themes from the perspective of the participant(s), then attempt to understand and explain these patterns and themes (Agar, 1980). During data analysis the data will be organized categorically and chronologically, reviewed repeatedly, and continually coded. A list of major ideas that surface will be chronicled (as suggested by Merriam, 1988). Taped interviews and the participant's taped diary will be transcribed verbatim. Field notes and diary entries will be regularly reviewed.

**(Assumptions are stated about data collection and coding.)**

In addition, the data analysis process will be aided by the use of a qualitative data analysis computer program called HyperQual. Raymond Padilla (Arizona State University) designed HyperQual in 1987 for use with the Macintosh computer. HyperQual utilizes HyperCard software and facilitates the recording and analysis of textual and graphic data. Special stacks are designated to hold and organize data. Using Hyper-Qual the researcher can directly "enter field data, including interview data, observations, researcher's memos, and illustrations . . . (and) tag (or code) all or part of the source data so that chunks of data can be pulled out and then be reassembled in a new and illuminating configuration" (Padilla, 1989, pp. 69-70). Meaningful data chunks can be identified, retrieved, isolated, grouped and regrouped for analysis. Categories or code names can be entered initially or at a later date. Codes can be added, changed or deleted with HyperQual editor and text can be searched for key categories, themes, words or phrases.

**(Software used in data analysis are mentioned.)**

*Verification*

In ensuring internal validity, the following strategies will be employed:

1. Triangulation of data—Data will be collected through multiple  sources to include interviews, observations and document analysis;

2. Member checking—The informant will serve as a check throughout the analysis process. An ongoing dialogue regarding my interpretations of the informant's reality and meanings will ensure the truth value of the data;

3. Long terms and repeated observations at the research site—Regular and repeated observations of similar phenomenon and settings will occur on-site over a four month period of time;

4. Peer examination—A doctoral student and graduate assistant in the Educational Psychology Department will serve as a peer examiner.

5. Participatory modes of research—The informant will be involved in most phases of this study, from the design of the project to checking interpretations and conclusions; and

6. Clarification of researcher bias—At the outset of this study researcher bias will be articulated in writing in the dissertation proposal under the heading "The Researcher's Role."

**(Internal validity in the study used by researcher.)**

The primary strategy utilized in this project to ensure external validity will be the provision of rich, thick, detailed descriptions so that anyone interested in transferability will have a solid framework for comparison (Merriam, 1988). Three techniques to ensure reliability will be employed in this study. First, the researcher will provide a detailed account of the focus of the study, the researcher's role, the informant's position and basis for selection, and the context from which data will be gathered (LeCompte & Goetz, 1984). Second, triangulation or multiple methods of data collection and analysis will be used, which strengthens reliability as well as internal validity (Merriam, 1988). Finally, data collection and analysis strategies will be reported in detail in order to provide a clear and accurate picture of the methods used in this study. All phases of this project will be subject to scrutiny by an external auditor who is experienced in qualitative research methods.

**(External validity in the study used by author.)**

*Reporting the Findings*

Lofland (1974) suggests that although data collection and analysis strategies are similar across qualitative methods, the way the findings are reported is diverse. Miles and Huberman (1984) address the importance of creating a data display and suggest that narrative text has been the most frequent form of display for qualitative data. This is a naturalistic study. Therefore, the results will be presented in descriptive, narrative

form rather than as a scientific report. Thick description will be the vehicle for communicating a holistic picture of the experiences of a new college president. The final project will be a construction of the informant's experiences and the meanings he attaches to them. This will allow readers to vicariously experience the challenges he encounters and provide a lens through which readers can view the subject's world. (pp. 23-37; used by permission from Miller)
**(Outcomes of the study are mentioned.)**

## SUMMARY

In this chapter I explored the design of a procedure for a qualitative research study. The design involves acknowledging that qualitative designs are based on different assumptions than quantitative designs. Also the specific type of qualitative design needs to be mentioned, recognizing that many types of designs are available to researchers. Researchers also should reflect on and express their role or experiences that will bias interpretations and bring a unique view to data collection and analysis. Approaches to data collection are mentioned, whether they include observations, interviews, document analysis, or analysis of visual materials. The procedure for recording information is also important to mention. Follow comments about data collection with thoughts about procedures of forming categories or themes and specific data analysis approaches identified with types of qualitative designs. Mention verification as the process whereby the researcher demonstrates internal validity, and discuss limited application of external validity and reliability. The final step is to identify the outcome for the study and provide the reader with a sense of the narrative form for the outcome and how this outcome compares and contrasts with theories and the literature.

# WRITING EXERCISES

1. Write a plan for the procedure to be used in your qualitative study. After writing the plan, use Table 9.1 as a checklist to determine the comprehensiveness of your plan.

2. Develop a rationale for why your study is best suited to be examined by using a qualitative approach, rather than a quantitative approach to research.

# ▼ *ADDITIONAL READINGS*

Bogdan, R. C., & Biklen, S. K. (1992). **Qualitative research for education: An introduction to theory and methods.** Boston: Allyn & Bacon.

Robert Bogdan and Sari Biklen provide chapters on collecting qualitative data, analyzing it, and writing the results. In the chapter on collecting data, the authors detail the procedures involved in compiling field notes: their types, content, and format. They suggest, in another chapter, useful compositional techniques in writing research. Examples of these techniques are the use of quotations, mixing analysis and examples, interpretations, and the use of multiple methods of presentations.

Fielding, N. G., & Lee, R. M. (1991). **Using computers in qualitative research.** Newbury Park, CA: Sage.

Nigel Fielding and Raymond Lee have edited a state-of-the-art book on computer applications in qualitative research. They cover many diverse topics, such as legal and ethical issues, the HyperText software program, and the use of automating qualitative data analysis. Reneta Tesch, in her chapter "Software for Qualitative Researchers: Analysis Needs and Program Capabilities," provides a useful condensed version of topics from her book (Tesch, 1990). The six analysis procedures available in most software programs (locating individual words and phrases, creating word lists, creating indexes, attaching key words to text segments, attaching codes to segments, and connecting codes) demonstrates the possibilities of computerized data analysis.

Marshall, C., & Rossman, G. B. (1989). **Designing qualitative research.** Newbury Park, CA: Sage.

Catherine Marshall and Gretchen Rossman provide one chapter on the "research approach" in which they describe important method issues. Their section on the researcher's role is especially helpful in addressing issues about entry into organizations through gatekeepers, and *reciprocity*, the idea that researchers should give back to informants for their assistance. This chapter, as well as others in the book, provides useful vignettes to demonstrate qualitative procedural issues.

Merriam, S. B. (1988). **Case study research in education: A qualitative approach.** San Francisco: Jossey-Bass.

Sharan Merriam identifies data collection and data analysis as two important phases of qualitative designs. Individual chapters are devoted to interviews, observations, and document analysis. In these chapters readers will find the advantages of each form of data collection and useful techniques for gathering information. In addition to a chapter on data analysis approaches, Merriam introduces the reader to the use of computers to analyze qualitative data. Especially helpful is yet another chapter on validity, reliability, and ethics. This discussion about validity and reliability is one of the best found in qualitative research texts.

Tesch, R. (1990). **Qualitative research: Analysis types and software tools.** New York: Falmer.

Reneta Tesch has compiled a text on qualitative data analysis that spans broad topics such as the types of qualitative designs, the mechanics of coding textual data, and computer software programs available for textual analysis. In her chapter "Types of Qualitative Research," complete with a graphic overview of 20 types of qualitative designs, she presents four categories of qualitative designs: the characteristics of language, the discovery of regularities, the comprehension of meaning of text/action, and reflection. This is the most detailed and comprehensible taxonomy of types to date. In her chapter "Organizing Systems and How to Develop Them" she provides a method for coding transcriptions. She also provides a useful discussion about qualitative software programs for textual data analysis.

# 10
▼

# *Combined Qualitative and Quantitative Designs*

In Chapter 1 I made the suggestion to identify a **single** paradigm—either qualitative or quantitative—for a research study. The reasons advanced were pragmatic, such as the extensive time required to use both paradigms adequately, the expertise needed by the researcher, the desire to limit the scope of a study, and the lengthy reporting requirements unsuitable for most journals. Assuming, for a moment, that these factors do not pose barriers for a researcher or a research team, how would one design a study that combines the qualitative and quantitative paradigms in a single study? To answer this question, I provide a brief overview about literature that addresses combining qualitative and quantitative research. Then

173

I present three models that advance useful prototypes for combining designs and suggest approaches for writing introductions, the literature and theory, the purpose statement and research questions/hypotheses, and the methods using each of the models. I end the chapter by reviewing three journal articles that illustrate each of the models.

## THE COMBINATION
## OF METHODS AND DESIGNS

The idea of combining qualitative and quantitative approaches in a single study owes much to past discussions about mixing methods, linking paradigms to methods, and combining research designs in all phases of a study. In terms of mixing methods, in 1959 Campbell and Fisk sought to use more than one method to measure a psychological trait to ensure that the variance was reflected in the trait and not in the method (see Brewer & Hunter, 1989, for a summary of Campbell and Fisk's multimethod-multitrait approach). By 1978 Denzin used the term *triangulation*, a term borrowed from navigation and military strategy, to argue for the combination of methodologies in the study of the same phenomenon. The concept of *triangulation* was based on the assumption that any bias inherent in particular data sources, investigator, and method would be neutralized when used in conjunction with other data sources, investigators, and methods (Jick, 1979). A combined method study is one in which the researcher uses multiple methods of data collection and analysis. These methods might be drawn from "within methods" approaches, such as different types of quantitative data collection strategies (e.g., a survey and an experiment). Alternatively it might involve "between methods," drawing on qualitative and quantitative data collection procedures (e.g., a survey and in-depth interviews) (Jick, 1979). Grant and Fine (1992), for example, cited numerous illustrations of combinations in the literature, ranging from observations supplemented with structured, quantitative observations, the mixing of ethnography and experimental research, and the successful combination of survey research and qualitative procedures.

Although triangulation was an important reason to combine qualitative and quantitative methods, recent authors have suggested additional reasons (Greene, Caracelli, & Graham, 1989; Mathison, 1988; Swanson, 1992). Greene et al. (1989) advanced five purposes for combining methods in a single study:

triangulation in the classic sense of seeking convergence of results

complimentary, in that overlapping and different facets of a phenomenon may emerge (e.g., peeling the layers of an onion)

developmentally, wherein the first method is used sequentially to help inform the second method

initiation, wherein contradictions and fresh perspectives emerge

expansion, wherein the mixed methods add scope and breadth to a study

Regardless of the purpose for combined methods, the concept of mixing methods raised an additional issue: Should paradigms be **linked** with methods? At issue was the question whether the paradigms **must** be linked with research methods. For example, if a researcher used an inductive, emerging qualitative stance in a study, does this mean that he or she must use qualitative data collection approaches such as observations and interviews? Alternatively, should a deductive, theory-driven study in the quantitative paradigm always be linked with quantitative data collection procedures such as surveys and experiments? The assumption behind linking paradigms with methods was that such an approach encouraged researchers to choose between quantitative and qualitative method types, rather than combine them (Reichardt & Cook, 1979). The use of multiple methods highlighted this issue, and the "paradigm debate" ensued (Guba, 1992; Patton, 1988).

Several schools of thinking arose in this debate. The "purists" said that paradigms and methods should not be mixed; the "situationalists" asserted that certain methods are appropriate for specific situations; and the "pragmatists" attempted to integrate methods in a single study (Rossman & Wilson, 1985; also see Lancy, 1993, for a typology of combining methods). The pragmatists argued that a false dichotomy existed between qualitative and quantitative approaches and that researchers should make the most efficient use of both paradigms in understanding social phenomena.

The most efficient use of both paradigms would suggest another step toward combining designs: Can aspects of the design process other than methods—such as the introduction to a study, the literature and theory, the purpose statement, and research questions— also be drawn from different paradigms in a single study? Here we have few studies as guides. The most substantive contribution in this area is the analysis by Greene et al. (1989). They began with the thought that "mixed-method designs remain largely uncharted" territory (p. 255). In a review of 57 evaluation studies conducted between 1980 and 1988, they not only identified several "purposes" for mixing methods but also explored the "design characteristics" (p. 263) that differentiated among the mixed-method models. They identified whether the **methods** selected for a given study were similar to or different from one another in form, assumptions, strengths, and limitations or biases. They also examined whether the methods were used to respond to **different questions.** They explored whether the different method types were implemented within the same or different **paradigms.** They looked at the **status** of the method: whether they had equal or unequal importance, given the overall objectives of the study. They finally examined the **implementation** of the study: whether the methods were implemented interactively, independently, concurrently, or sequentially. Greene et al. (1989) continued on to relate these "design" features to their mixed-method types. They stopped short of suggesting how one might combine the two paradigms at all phases in the design process.

## MODELS OF COMBINED DESIGNS

Given this background, I now advance three models of combined designs that I have found in the literature:

▼ *It is advantageous to a researcher to combine methods to better understand a concept being tested or explored.*

▼ *Consider integrating the paradigms at several phases of the research process.*

▼ *Use the two-phase design, the dominant-less dominant design, or the mixed-methodology design to combine qualitative and quantitative approaches in a single study.*

The first model I call the **two-phase design** approach, in which the researcher proposes to conduct a qualitative phase of the study and a separate quantitative phase of the study. The advantage of this approach is that the two paradigms are clearly separate; it also enables a researcher to present thoroughly the paradigm assumptions behind each phase. The disadvantage is that the reader may not discern the connection between the two phases.

The second model I call the **dominant-less dominant design.** In this design the researcher presents the study within a single, dominant paradigm with one small component of the overall study drawn from the alternative paradigm. A classic example of this approach is a quantitative study based on testing a theory in an experiment with a small qualitative interview component in the data collection phase. Alternatively one might engage in qualitative observations with a limited number of informants, followed by a quantitative survey of a sample from a population. The advantage of this approach is that it presents a consistent paradigm picture in the study and still gathers limited information to probe in detail one aspect of the study. The chief disadvantage is that qualitative purists would see this approach as misusing the qualitative paradigm because the central assumptions of the study would not link or match the qualitative data collection procedure. Quantitative purists also would be concerned about the match.

The third model is the **mixed-methodology design.** This design represents the highest degree of mixing paradigms of the three designs. The researcher would mix aspects of the qualitative and quantitative paradigm at all or many methodological steps in the design. The paradigms might be mixed in the introduction, in the literature review and theory use, and in the purpose statement and the research questions. This approach adds complexity to a design and uses the advantages of both the qualitative and the quantitative paradigms. Moreover, the overall design perhaps best mirrors the research process of working back and forth between inductive and deductive models of thinking in a research study. On the negative side it requires a sophisticated knowledge of both paradigms, conveys the linking of paradigms that may be unacceptable to some authors, and requires that the writer convey a combination of paradigms unfamiliar to many researchers.

## THE MODELS AND DESIGN PHASES

To illustrate each of the models, I relate them to the phases in research design presented in prior chapters in this book. The discussion addresses writing an introduction to a study, using the literature and theory, writing a purpose statement and research questions or hypotheses, and describing the methods and findings to a study.

### The Introduction

As mentioned in Chapter 3, subtle differences exist between the qualitative and quantitative designs of an introduction. In a **qualitative** study one would find minimal literature—enough to discuss the problem; language to suggest an emerging design and words to convey that the researcher hopes to understand, discover, develop a theory; and perhaps the use of the personal voice through pronouns in the writing. Alternatively, in **quantitative** introductions one finds a firm grounding in the literature, a theory advanced that one wishes to test, and the impersonal voice of writing.

In the **two-phase design** the researcher would introduce a qualitative phase and a quantitative phase of the study. Typically this presentation might take the form of introducing a two-phase project. An alternative design is to present two introductions, spaced apart in the presentation, with each introducing a separate phase of the study.

In the **dominant-less dominant design** the researcher would present the introduction from the framework of the dominant paradigm in the study. For instance, in a quantitative-dominant study the writer might advance an **a priori** theory to be tested and use the impersonal voice. In a **mixed-methodology design** the introduction might be presented in the approach consistent with either paradigm, but the author would suggest explicitly that the study will be based on both paradigms. As recommended by Patton (1991), the researcher should "keep his or her assumptions explicit at all times" (p. 392).

### The Literature and Theory

The use of literature and theory should be consistent with the paradigm being used by the researcher. In Chapters 2 and 6 I suggested that theory and literature be used inductively in **qualitative** studies, be introduced in the emerging design toward the end of a study, and be positioned in a limited sense in the beginning of the study to "frame" the problem. In **quantitative** studies, however, theory and literature are used deductively, are advanced to help guide the study and the development of research questions, and are discussed at some length in the beginning of a study. How would these characteristics apply to the three models?

In a **two-phase design** the literature and theory would be used inductively in a qualitative phase of the study and deductively in the quantitative phase. An exception, of course, is the qualitative designs with a strong theory-orientation, such as critical ethnography. In the **dominant-less dominant design** the literature and theory would be used in an approach consistent with the dominant paradigm (inductive in qualitative; deductive in quantitative). As suggested by Morse (1991), "A project must be theoretically driven by the qualitative methods incorporating a complementary quantitative component, or theoretically driven by the quantitative method, incorporating a complementary qualitative component"

(p. 121). In a **mixed-methodology design** it is difficult, if not impossible, to mix the two paradigms in the use of theory and the literature. Despite the apparent incompatibility of an inductive versus deductive approach to research, one finds **in practice** theory and literature used without a strict interpretation of the inductive and deductive associations with the paradigms. Thus it is possible to use theory and the literature in modes unassociated with accepted approaches of their paradigms. The following examples illustrate some of these forms.

Write the theory into the beginning of the study in a qualitative project. This approach would challenge the inductive approach in a qualitative study but would combine a quantitative use of theory in a qualitative study. Moreover, the theory would be introduced, not as a series of propositions to be tested, but as a series of propositions to be modified. An example of this model is found in Murguia et al. (1991). They introduced Tinto's model in the introduction of the study but stated they thought the model was "incompletely conceptualized" and sought, through the qualitative study, to improve and modify the model.

In a quantitative project, present the theory at the beginning as a tentative model or conceptualization to be developed and refined during data collection (Miles & Huberman, 1984). This approach is contrary to the deductive model in a good quantitative design. It advances an emerging theoretical orientation within a quantitative project.

Write a substantial literature review, even a separate "review of the literature" section into the introduction of a qualitative study. This model suggests a quantitative orientation to the literature in a qualitative study. This approach appears frequently in qualitative studies, especially in studies reported in journals aimed toward more quantitatively oriented audiences. For example, in Mandell's (1984) symbolic interaction study of children's negotiation of meaning, she provided an extensive review of the literature at the outset of the study. Her literature review on research on childhood socialization and role taking was presented within a symbolic interaction qualitative design.

Design a literature review for a qualitative study that organizes the subtopics around the literature published on the grand tour questions and subquestions in the study. This approach uses a quantitative model for organizing the literature as discussed in Chapter 2. Rather than use the quantitative independent, dependent, and independent-dependent studies as a framework, the qualitative researcher would use the grand tour questions and subquestions as a framework for deciding on the appropriate sections for the review of the literature.

Review both qualitative and quantitative studies in a review of the literature in qualitative and quantitative studies. One might make explicit the understanding of the assumptions of both paradigms by grouping qualitative studies together and quantitative studies together (and labeling them accordingly). Alternatively the researcher might identify the paradigm assumptions associated with each study.

## Purpose Statement and
## Research Questions/Hypotheses

The purpose statement and research questions in a **qualitative** study, as discussed in Chapters 4 and 5, are designed to be open-ended, descriptive, and nondirectional. In a **quantitative** design they are directional and state a relationship or comparison, specify a multivariate relationship between independent and dependent variables, and relate to a theoretical perspective.

In the **two-phase design** model two sets of purpose statements and research questions are presented, each in the phase to which they apply. Their form represents the characteristics of the paradigm used in the phase. For instance, the qualitative characteristics are written into the qualitative phase of the study. The **dominant-less dominant design** would use a purpose statement and questions/hypotheses posed in the language of the dominant design. Perhaps a secondary purpose (and questions/hypotheses) would be described in the language of the less-dominant design. This approach implies a sequence, as well as a weighting, of the two designs.

Morse (1991) illustrated the use of shorthand labels for qualitative and quantitative research questions and a sequence for ordering the two designs. She contended that the two paradigms cannot be weighted equally in a single study and assigned capital and small letters (e.g., QUANT or quant) to signify the weight given to a paradigm in a study. Morse further suggested that "methodological triangulation" can occur between qualitative and quantitative approaches in two ways: by simultaneous triangulation or by sequential triangulation. In **simultaneous triangulation** the researcher answers the qualitative and quantitative research questions at the same time in the study. Results to the qualitative questions, for example, would be reported separately and would not necessarily relate to or confirm the results from the quantitative study. In **sequential triangulation** the researcher conducts two phases of the project, with the results of the first phase essential for planning the next phase. The first questions of Phase 1 are completed before the questions of Phase 2 are raised. She illustrated these approaches:

*Example 1.   Simultaneous Triangulation*

### QUAL + quan Illustration

What is it like to be a relative of a patient in the ICU? This is clearly a qualitative problem, and the methods of ethnography or grounded theory may be used to describe the experience of anxious, waiting relatives. From the inception of the project, we can quite safely assume that the relative will be anxious. But how anxious? Clearly, it would strengthen our description of the sample if we could administer a standardized anxiety scale and include a description of the levels of anxiety that relatives may be experiencing.

### QUAN + qual Illustration

The conceptual framework of this study predicts that the sicker the child, the greater the spatial distance between the

parents and the child; and the greater the spatial distance between the parents and the child, the greater the child's anxiety.
How do we measure spatial distance in this situation? One way
would be to do participant observation at randomly selected
intervals: another way would be to use video cameras to observe
the distance between the parents and their child. (p. 121)

*Example 2. Sequential Triangulation*

**QUAL** – *quan Illustration*

A qualitative study on the responses of adolescents to menarche
provided many insights into adolescent behavior and their affective response to menstruation at this time. But what were
the normative attitudes of adolescent girls towards menarche?
The domains from the content analysis were used to construct
a Likert scale, and the items were derived directly from the
qualitative data. Quantitative methods of ensuring reliability
and validity were used, and the Likert Scale was administered
to a randomly selected sample.

**QUAN** – *qual Illustration*

A large infant feeding survey of a Third World country produced the unexpected finding that there was no difference in
the incidence of infantile diarrhea in infants from homes with
or without refrigeration. Qualitative interviews with a sample
of residents from homes with refrigerators revealed that infant formula bottles were not kept in the refrigerator. Refrigerators were used for making and storing ice, which was sold
to supplement the family income. (p. 121).

These four models illustrate several possibilities for writing research
questions giving different weight to the paradigms in the design.

In the **mixed-methodology design** the researcher could present
two purposes for the study—one qualitative and one quantitative—
and present them in the language characteristic of both paradigms.
Moreover, the research questions could be advanced by first presenting descriptive questions (grand tour questions and subquestions)

for the qualitative component of the study and multivariate questions (comparing groups or relating variables) for the quantitative
approach. In fact, a variation on this model is presented in Chapter 5, for writing **quantitative** research questions. The distinction
would be that in the mixed-methodology design the descriptive
questions follow more closely the characteristics of good qualitative questions rather than descriptive questions focused on the
independent and dependent variables as discussed in Chapter 5.

*The Methods*

In the section on **quantitative** methods to data collection in
Chapter 8, I discussed survey procedures and experimental designs.
The information collected through these procedures was analyzed
statistically to generalize from the data and support or refute theories.
In **qualitative** approaches in Chapter 9 I presented four common
types of data collection: observations, interviews, documents, and
visual material. The analysis of these sources of information follows
a general model of deriving themes or categories from particulars
and developing a qualitative narrative that presents a pattern or a
larger picture through multiple levels of analysis.

In the **two-phase design** the methods and the result of the
qualitative phase of the study are reported separately from the
methods and results of the qualitative phase. One would expect to
find separate headings in the study. The intent of the two-phase
project is, in all probability, to triangulate or converge the findings,
and a separate section might address this issue after both phases
are discussed. In a **dominant-less dominant design** the methods and
results relate to the dominant paradigm in use, with a small segment
for methods and results for the less-dominant paradigm. In the
illustration in which a major quantitative study is undertaken,
supplemented by a few qualitative interviews, the researcher may
hope to elaborate, enhance, or illustrate the results from one method
by using another method. In a **mixed-methodological design**
study, one finds "mixed methods" presented where the author collects
both qualitative and quantitative data. Both themes and statistical
analysis are presented. In Rossman and Wilson's (1985) terms, an
"integrated" use of methods exists. Also the mixed methods may

have several purposes: triangulating or converging findings, elaborating on results, using one method to inform another, discovering paradox or contradiction, and extending the breadth of the inquiry (Greene et al., 1989).

## EXAMPLES

Below I illustrate the three design possibilities with studies from the literature.

*Example 3.   A Two-Phase Design*

Kushman (1992) studied two types of teacher workplace commitment—organizational commitment and commitment to student learning—in 63 urban elementary and middle schools. He posed a two-phase methodology:

> The central premise of this study was that organizational commitment and commitment to student learning address distinct but equally important teacher attitudes for an organizationally effective school, an idea that has some support in the literature but requires further empirical validation. . . . Phase 1 was a quantitative study that looked at statistical relationships between teacher commitment and organizational antecedents and outcomes in elementary and middle schools. Following this macrolevel analysis, Phase 2 looked within specific schools, using qualitative/case study methods to better understand the dynamics of teacher commitment. (Kushman, 1992, p. 13)

The introduction is not presented in two phases: It examines the problem leading to the study and focuses on the purpose of the study, to examine organizational commitment and commitment to student learning. This introduction is followed by sections defining organizational commitment and commitment to student learning. Extensive literature is used to document these two concepts. A conceptual framework then follows (complete with a visual model), and research questions are posed to explore relationships. These aspects of the study all suggest a dominant quantitative approach, except that the author then presents the two phases to the study—first the quantitative phase, and next the qualitative phase. Results also are presented in terms of phases. The quantitative results present correlations, regressions, and two-way ANOVAs. Then the case study results are presented in terms of themes and subthemes supported by quotes. The final discussion highlights the quantitative results and the complexities that surfaced from the qualitative results. In the final analysis, this study shows a two-design model, albeit limited to the method, results, and discussion sections. Both phases are of equal stature, and the study has all the advantages of an extensive use of each paradigm of research and the limitation of a clear convergence of the results from both phases of the design.

*Example 4. A Dominant-Less Dominant Design*

Hofstede, Neuijen, Ohayv, and Sanders (1990) studied organizational cultures in 20 units from 10 different organizations in Denmark and the Netherlands. The study consisted of three phases, with one phase based on in-depth interviews "to get a qualitative feel for the gestalt of the unit's culture and to collect issues to be included in the questionnaire" (p. 290). The second and third phases consisted of surveys. After briefly presenting descriptions from interviews for two units from two organizations, the authors analyzed extensively the survey information in a section called "Results." This section included extensive statistical hypothesis testing.

This study represents a dominant quantitative approach with a less-dominant qualitative data collection procedure. In a quantitatively oriented introduction, the authors review the literature on organizational cultures and summarize past research on national cultures. From this introduction they move directly into the methods and identify the three phases. They next present two mini-case studies of two organizations and follow these cases with detailed information about the survey questionnaire and data analysis. From this point on, the results are presented quantitatively, with statistical tests about the differences in the cultures of the organizations. In summary, the qualitative aspect of this study was limited to two mini-case studies; other components of the design were quantitative, leading one to conclude that the overall design was dominated by the quantitative paradigm.

*Example 5.   A Mixed-Methodology Design*

In Gogolin and Swartz's (1992) "A Quantitative and Qualitative Inquiry Into the Attitudes Toward Science of Nonscience College Students" one sees a combination of qualitative and quantitative approaches throughout the study. The authors studied the attitudes toward science of 102 nonscience and 81 science majors in a college. They posed three questions: How attitudes toward science of nonscience college students compared with attitudes of science major; whether attitudes toward science change with instruction; and attitude development as it relates to science. They measured six attitudinal variables by using the Attitudes Toward Science Inventory. They collected interview information by means of an interview questionnaire containing closed-ended and open-ended items. After taking a science course, the science and nonscience students were compared in terms of the inventory at the pretest and posttest stages. A statistically significant difference was found in these scores for the nonscience students. Results indicated a favorable change in attitude toward science. As a second aspect of the study, the researchers interviewed 25 randomly selected nonscience students. Four themes about attitudes toward science emerged from these interviews: home environment, school environment, peer relationship, and self-concept. Implications of these quantitative and qualitative results were discussed by the authors.

A concept map of the flow of qualitative and quantitative ideas in this article is shown in Figure 10.1. The ideas encircled by double lines indicate the major sections that unfold in the study. The authors begin with an introduction, move on to related research, advance the methods from both the qualitative and quantitative data collection phase, discuss quantitative results followed by qualitative results, present a discussion summarizing the quantitative and qualitative results separately, and then end the article with an implication section wherein they also discuss the qualitative and quantitative implications separately.

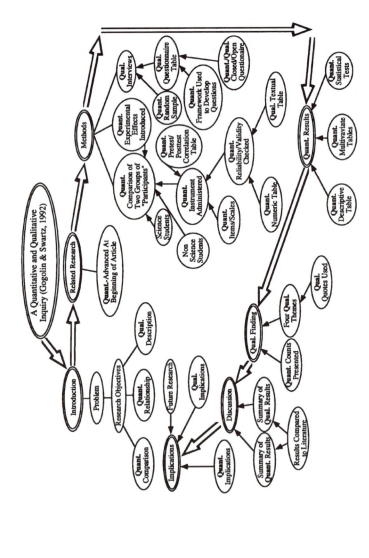

**Figure 10.1.** A Concept Map of the Quantitative and Qualitative Study by Gogolin & Swartz (1992)

SOURCE: Data from "A Quantitative and Qualitative Inquiry Into the Attitudes Toward Science of Nonscience College Students" by L. Gogolin and F. Swartz, 1992, *Journal of Research in Science Teaching, 29*.

The flow of ideas in this study shows several stages in the design where both quantitative and qualitative approaches were used. The introduction advances objectives related to description (qualitative), as well as comparison and relationships (quantitative). The methods involve comparing groups in terms of experimental effects (quantitative), as well as interviews (qualitative). The results are interpreted for the quantitative data (statistical tests) and the qualitative data (themes). The discussion summarizes both quantitative and qualitative results, and implications are drawn from both results. In summary, in almost all phases of the research, the authors include elements of the qualitative and quantitative approaches to research.

## SUMMARY

The discussion to this point has addressed the design of qualitative and quantitative studies as distinct, separate designs. In this chapter I discussed approaches to combining designs in a single study. Discussions about combining qualitative and quantitative approaches focused on "mixed methods," wherein the original intent was to "triangulate" findings, to demonstrate convergence in results. More recently, authors have broadened the purposes for mixing methods to include an examination of overlapping and different facets, to use the methods sequentially, to find contradictions and new perspectives, and to add scope and breadth to a study.

Mixing methods from qualitative and quantitative traditions has contributed to discussions about their value, especially because they raise the question of the operative paradigm being used. Whether paradigms should be linked with methods has led to different schools of thinking. Mixing methods also has raised a methodological issue as to whether the other "design" components of a study should follow one paradigm approach or the other.

I advanced three design models: the two-phase design, in which the qualitative and quantitative studies are presented and discussed in two distinct phases; the dominant-less dominant design, in which one paradigm dominates the study and a less paradigm is used, typically in the data collection phase; and the mixed-methodology design, in which the research combines qualitative and quantitative approaches throughout the study, such as in the introduction, the purpose statement, the research questions, and the methods.

# WRITING EXERCISES

1. Design a combined qualitative and quantitative study that employs two phases. Discuss why the phases are ordered in the sequence you propose.

2. Design a combined qualitative and quantitative study that uses a dominant qualitative component and a less-dominant quantitative component. Discuss the approach to be taken in writing the introduction, the purpose statement, the research questions, and the methods.

3. Design a combined qualitative and quantitative study that employs a mixed-methodological approach. Present this design as a visual diagram (or concept map) and identify the qualitative and quantitative components in the design.

## ▼ ADDITIONAL READINGS

Greene, J. C., Caracelli, V. J., & Graham, W. F. (1989). Toward a conceptual framework for mixed-method evaluation designs. **Educational Evaluation and Policy Analysis,** 11(3), 255-274.

Jennifer Greene and associates undertook a study of 57 mixed-method evaluation studies reported from 1980 to 1988. From this analysis they developed five mixed-method purposes and seven design characteristics. They found the purposes of mixed-method studies to be based on seeking convergence (triangulation), on examining different facets of a phenomena (complementarity), on using the methods sequentially (development), on discovering paradox and fresh perspectives (initiation), and on adding breadth and scope to a project (expansion). They also found that the studies varied in terms of the assumptions, strengths, and limitations of the method and whether they addressed different phenomena or the same phenomena; were implemented within the same or different paradigms; were given equal or different weight in the study; and were implemented independently or concurrently or sequentially. Using the purposes and the design characteristics, the authors recommend several mixed-method designs.

Jick, T. D. (1979). Mixing qualitative and quantitative methods: Triangulation in action. **Administrative Science Quarterly,** 24, 602-611.

Todd Jick provides a historical sketch of triangulation and illustrates the use of triangulation in a study of the effects of a merger on employees. *Triangulation,* according to Jick, is the combination of methodologies in the same study. He presents a continuum of triangulation design from simple scaling to a holistic contextual design. Regardless of design, triangulation rests on the assumption that the weakness in a single method will be compensated by the strengths of another method. Triangulation therefore exploits the assets and neutralizes the liabilities of different methods. Jick ends his article with an illustration of the practice of triangulation and how the quantitative results supplemented the qualitative data.

Mathison, S. (1988). Why triangulate? **Educational Researcher,** 17(2), 13-17.

Sandra Mathison challenges the traditional meaning of *triangulation* that typically refers to improving the validity of research by using a variety of methods. One assumption of triangulation is that bias inherent in data sources, investigators, and methods will be canceled out when used in conjunction with other sources, investigators, and methods. A second assumption is that triangulation of results will provide convergence about the "truth" of some social phenomenon. Mathison outlines an alternative strategy for triangulation that provides better evidence for researchers. This strategy involves using a variety of methods to look for convergence, inconsistency, and contradictory evidence.

Morse, J. M. (1991). Approaches to qualitative-quantitative methodological triangulation. **Nursing Research,** 40(1), 120-123.

Janice Morse argues that using qualitative and quantitative methods to address the same research problem leads to issues of weighing each method and their sequence in a study. From these ideas, she then advances two forms of methodological triangulation: *simultaneous,* using both methods at the same time, and *sequential,* using the results of one method for planning the next method. Further, these two forms can be described by a notation of capital and small letters that signify the relative weight given to a method as well as sequence. For example, sequential triangulation is indicated by QUAL ———- quan, suggesting that the project is inductive and based on a qualitative foundation. The different approaches to triangulation then are discussed in light of their purpose, limitations, and approaches.

# 11
▼

# *Scholarly Writing*

The plan for a scholarly dissertation or journal article is a written document. As such, it must convince others of the worth of a study in a clear and concise manner. It is the prelude to the final study, and it needs to mirror the probable strength of the final written document.

From the preceding chapters it should be evident that I have incorporated thoughts from my interest in composition and scholarly writing. Now I make explicit these thoughts, drawing on my favorite writing books and sharing ideas that have worked well for me. Most of the ideas in this chapter apply equally well to qualitative and quantitative approaches.

I begin the chapter with more macro-level writing strategies and conclude with micro-level applications. Some approaches are familiar territory for those reading books about writing. A section on "writing as thinking" provides suggestions for writing early in the process of research and revising and editing multiple drafts. Then "habit of writing" offers ideas about the physical setting and the critical "warm-up" necessary as an antecedent to writing. A highly readable manuscript should be the outcome of the writing process, and coherence is built into a study by using consistent terms, staging narrative thoughts, and connecting sentences and paragraphs. In addition, using the appropriate narrative voice, attending to verb tense, and trimming the "fat" from prose are all useful techniques. I end the discussion with a brief discussion about the use of computer phrase-checking programs.

## WRITING AS THINKING

One sign of an inexperienced writer is that he or she prefers to discuss the proposed study, rather than to write about it. All experienced writers know that writing is thinking and conceptualizing a topic. I recommend the following:

▼ *Early in the process of research, write down ideas, rather than talk about them.* The writing specialists of today see the writing process as the thinking process (Bailey, 1984). Zinsser (1983) discusses the need to get words out of our heads and onto paper. I react better, for example, when I look at the printed text on paper than when I discuss a research topic with a colleague or a student. By rendering the ideas to paper, I can visualize the final product, "see" how it looks on paper, and begin clarifying ideas. The concept of working out ideas on paper has served well many experienced writers.

▼ *Work through several drafts of a paper, rather than try to polish the first draft.* It is illuminating to see how people think on paper. Zinsser (1983) identified two types of writers: the "brick-layer," who makes every paragraph just right before going on to the next paragraph, and the "let-it-all-hang-out-on-the-first-draft" writer, who writes an entire first draft not caring how sloppy it looks or how badly it is written. In between would be someone like Peter Elbow (1973), who recommends that one should go through the iterative process of writing, reviewing, and rewriting. For example, with only an hour to write a passage, write four drafts (one each in 15 minutes), rather than one draft (typically in the last 15 minutes). Most experienced researchers write the first draft carefully but do not work for a polished draft; the polish comes relatively late in the writing process. For instance, Franklin (1986) recommends a three-stage model for writing that provides useful advice for the scholarly writer:

First, develop an outline—it could be a sentence or word outline or a visual map of ideas.

Second, develop a draft and work on the structural components of a manuscript by shifting and sorting ideas and by moving around entire paragraphs in the manuscript.

Third, work on polishing the sentences.

## THE HABIT OF WRITING

▼ *Establish the writing process—the discipline of writing on a continuous and regular basis.* Setting aside the manuscript for long periods of time results in loss of concentration and effort. I say "the writing process" because the actual writing of words on a page is only part of the process of thinking, collecting information, and reviewing that goes into manuscript production.

▼ *Establish good writing habits.* Select a time of day best for working. Then use discipline to write at this time each day. Choose a place free of distractions. Boice (1990) offers ideas about establishing good writing habits:

1. With the aid of the priority principle, make writing a daily activity, regardless of mood, regardless of readiness to write.
2. If you feel you do not have time for regular writing, begin by charting your daily activities for a week or two in half-hour blocks.
3. Write while you are fresh.
4. Avoid writing in binges.
5. Write in small, regular amounts.

6. Schedule writing tasks so that you plan to work on specific, finishable units of writing in each session.

7. Keep daily charts. Graph at least three things: (a) time spent writing, (b) page equivalents finished, and (c) percentage of planned task completed.

8. Plan beyond daily goals.

9. Share your writing with supportive, constructive friends before you feel ready to go public.

10. Try to work on two or three writing projects concurrently. (Boice, 1990, pp. 77-78)

▼ *In addition to these thoughts, one needs to acknowledge that writing moves along slowly and to ease into writing.* Like the exerciser who stretches before a road race, the writer needs warm-up exercises for both the mind and the fingers. Some leisurely writing activity, such as writing a letter to a friend, brain-storming on the computer, or reading some good writing or a favorite poem, can make the actual task of writing easier. I am reminded of John Steinbeck's (1969) "warm-up period" (p. 42) described in detail in *Journal of a Novel: The East of Eden Letters.* Steinbeck began each writing day by writing a letter to his editor and close friend, Pascal Covici, in a large notebook supplied by Covici.

Other exercises may prove useful. Carroll (1990) provides examples of exercises to improve a writer's control over descriptive and emotive passages:

Describe an object by its parts and dimensions, without first telling the reader its name.

Write a conversation between two people on any dramatic or intriguing subject.

Write a set of directions for a complicated task.

Take a subject and write about it in three different ways. (Carroll, 1990, pp. 113-116)

This last exercise seems appropriate for qualitative researchers who need to decide on their point of view in a study (see Chap. 3, on alternatives for writing an introduction).

Consider also the implements of writing and the physical location that aid the process of disciplined writing. The implements of writing—a typewriter, a computer, a yellow legal-sized pad, a favorite pen, even a pencil—each offers a comfort level, and researchers need to find the best writing device. The physical setting for writing also can help. Annie Dillard, the Pulitzer prize-winning novelist, avoids appealing workplaces:

> One wants a room with no view, so imagination can meet memory in the dark. When I furnished this study seven years ago, I pushed the long desk against a blank wall, so I could not see from either window. Once, fifteen years ago, I wrote in a cinder-block cell over a parking lot. It overlooked a tar-and-gravel roof. This pine shed under trees is not quite so good as the cinder-block study was, but it will do. (Dillard, 1989, pp. 26-27)

## READABILITY OF THE MANUSCRIPT

How quickly and smoothly does the manuscript read? In the preceding chapters I suggested use of consistent terms, a staging of ideas, and a coherence built into the plan.

▼ *Use **consistent** terms throughout the manuscript.* Stay with the same term each time a variable is mentioned in a quantitative study or a key concept is mentioned in a qualitative study. Refrain from using synonyms for these terms, a problem that causes the reader to work at understanding the meaning of ideas and to monitor subtle shifts in meaning.

▼ *Consider how narrative "thoughts" of different types guide a reader.* This concept was advanced by Tarshis (1982), who recommended that writers stage "thoughts" to guide readers. These were of four types:

Umbrella thoughts. The general or core ideas one is trying to get across.

Big thoughts. Specific ideas or images that fall within the realm of umbrella thoughts and serve to reinforce, clarify, or elaborate on the umbrella thoughts.

Little thoughts. Ideas or images whose chief function is to reinforce big thoughts.

Attention or interest thoughts. Ideas whose purpose is to keep the reader on track, organize ideas, and keep an individual's attention.

Beginning researchers, I believe, struggle most with "umbrella" thoughts and "attention" thoughts. A manuscript may include too many "umbrella" ideas, with the content not sufficiently detailed to support large ideas. A clear mark of this problem is a continual shift of ideas from one major idea to another in a manuscript. Often one will see short paragraphs, almost like those found written by journalists in newspaper articles. Thinking in terms of a detailed narrative to support umbrella ideas may help this problem. Goldberg (1986) not only talks about the power of detail but also illustrates it using the example of the Vietnam veterans memorial in Washington D.C., where names—even middle names—of 50,000 killed American soldiers are listed.

Lack of "attention" thoughts also derail a good narrative. Readers need "road signs" to guide them from one major idea to the next. They need to see the overall organization of the ideas through introductory paragraphs and to be told, in a summary, the most salient points they should remember.

▼ Use **coherence** to add *to the readability of the manuscript*. In presenting the topics in this book, I have introduced the components of the research process to present a systematic whole. For example, the repetition of variables in the title, the purpose statement, the research questions, and the review of the literature heading in a quantitative project illustrates this thinking. This approach builds **coherence** into the study. Furthermore, by emphasizing a consistent order of variables whenever independent and dependent variables are mentioned in quantitative studies also reinforces this idea.

On a more detailed level, **coherence** builds through connecting sentences and paragraphs in the manuscript. Zinsser (1983) suggests that every sentence should be a logical sequel to the one that preceded it. A useful exercise is the "hook-and-eye" exercise for connecting thoughts from sentence to sentence (or paragraph to paragraph).

The following passage from a draft of a student's dissertation proposal shows a high level of coherence. It is taken from the introductory section to a qualitative dissertation proposal about at-risk students. In this passage I have taken the liberty of drawing "hooks" and "eyes" to connect the ideas from sentence to sentence and from paragraph to paragraph. The objective of the hook-and-eye exercise (Wilkinson, 1991) is to connect major thoughts of each sentence. If such a connection cannot be made easily, the written passage lacks coherence and the writer needs to add transitional words, phrases, or sentences to establish a clear connection.

*Example 1.   A Sample Passage Illustrating the Hook-and-Eye Technique*

They sit in the back of the room not because they want to but because it was the place designated to them. Invisible barriers that exist in most classrooms divide the room and separate the students. At the front of the room are the "good" students, who wait with their hands poised ready to fly into the air at a moment's notice. Slouched down like giant insects caught in educational traps, the athletes and their following occupy the center of the room. Those less sure of themselves and their position within the room sit in the back and around the edge of the student body.

The students seated in the outer circle make up a population whom for a variety of reasons are not succeeding in the American public education system. They have always been part of the student population. In the past they have been called disadvantaged, low achieving, retards, impoverished, laggards and a variety of other titles (Cuban, 1989; Presseisen, 1988).

Today they are called students-at-risk. Their faces are changing and in urban settings their numbers are growing
(Hodgkinson, 1985).

In the past eight years there has been an unprecedented
amount of research on the need for excellence in education
and the at-risk student. In 1983 the government released a
document entitled *A Nation at Risk* that identified problems
within the American education system and called for major
reform. Much of the early reform focused on more vigorous
courses of study and higher standards of student achievement
(Barber, 1987). In the midst of attention to excellence, it became
apparent the needs of the marginal student were not being
met. The question of what it would take to guarantee that all
students have a fair chance at a quality education was receiving
little attention (Hamilton, 1987; Toch, 1984). As the push for
excellence in education increased, the needs of the at-risk student became more apparent.

Much of the early research focused on identifying characteristics of the at-risk student (OERI, 1987; Barber & McClellan,
1987; Hahn, 1987; Rumberger, 1987), while others in educational research called for reform and developed programs for
at-risk students (Mann, 1987; Presseisen, 1988; Whelage,
1988; Whelege & Lipman, 1988; Stocklinski, 1991; and Levin,
1991). Studies and research on this topic have included experts
within the field of education, business and industry as well as
many government agencies.

Although progress has been made in identifying characteristics of the at-risk students and in developing programs to
meet their needs, the essence of the at-risk issue continues to
plague the American school system. Some educators feel that
we do not need further research (DeBlois, 1989; Hahn, 1987).
Others call for a stronger network between business and education (DeBlois, 1989; Mann, 1987; Whelege, 1988). Still others call for total restructuring of our education system (OERI,
1987; Gainer, 1987; Levin, 1988; McCune, 1988).

After all the research and studies by the experts, we still
have students hanging on to the fringe of education. The
uniqueness of this study will shift the focus from causes and
curriculum to the student. It is time to question the students
and to listen to their responses. This added dimension should
bring further understanding to research already available and

lead to further areas of reform. Dropouts and potential dropouts will be interviewed in depth to discover if there are common factors within the public school setting that interfere
with their learning process. This information should be helpful to both the researcher who will continue to look for new
approaches in education and the practitioner who works with
these students everyday.


## VOICE, TENSE, AND FAT

From working with broad thoughts and paragraphs, I move on
to the sentence and word level of writing. In Franklin's (1986)
terms, one now is working at the "polish" level of writing, a stage
addressed late in the writing process. Writing books abound with
rules and principles to follow about good sentence construction and
word choice. The following ideas about active voice, verb tense,
and reduced "fat" strengthen and invigorate scholarly writing.

▼ *Use the active voice as much as possible in scholarly writing.*
According to Ross-Larson (1982), "If the subject acts, the voice
is active. If the subject is acted on, the voice is passive" (p. 29).
In addition, a sign of passive construction is some variation
of an auxiliary verb, such as *was, will be, have been,* and *is
being.*

Computer phrase-checking programs call these words "to be"
verbs. For example, the following sentences illustrate (rather than
"were written in") the passive voice:

*Example 2.  Active and Passive Voice*

Passive:   This book was written by me.
Active:   I wrote the book.
Passive:   The results were reported in a recent study.
Active:   Smith (1985) reported results about the study.

Writers can use the passive construction when the person acting
can logically be left out of the sentence and when what is acted on

is the subject of the rest of the paragraph (Ross-Larson, 1982). The following two examples illustrate these exceptions.

*Example 3.   Appropriate Use of Passive Construction When the Person Acting Can Logically Be Left Out*

> Self-esteem was found to be positively related to type of cloth-ing worn by the subjects.

(In this example, one does not want to repeat the words "the researcher" over and over in the results section of a manuscript.)

*Example 4.   Appropriate Use of Passive Construction When What Is Acted On Is the Subject of the Rest of the Paragraph*

> This research explored the relationship between individual self-esteem and clothing type among American teenagers. Self-esteem was found to be positively related to type of clothing worn by the subject.

(In this example, from the first sentence we know that the research explored a relationship. We do not have to make this point explicit in the second sentence.)

> ▼ *Use strong verbs and verb tenses appropriate for the passage in the study.* Lazy verbs are those that lack action (e.g., *is, was*) or those used as adjectives or adverbs. For example, verbs might be used as adjectives:

*Example 5.   A Verb Used as an Adjective*

Poor model:   Finally reaching statistical significance, the rela-tionship was highlighted.

Better model:   The relationship reached statistical significance.

A common practice is to use the past tense to review the literature and to report results of a study. The future tense would be appropriate at all other times in research proposals and plans (hence, I suggest, in Chap. 4, the use of *will* in describing the "purpose statement"). For completed studies, use the past tense to add vigor to a study, especially in the introduction. And avoid the use of anthropomorphic verbs, giving nouns humanlike characteristics, such as "The study spoke about the effects of criticism."

▼ *Expect to edit and revise drafts of a manuscript to trim excess words, the "fat," from the prose.* Writing multiple drafts of a manuscript is standard practice for most writers. The process typically consists of writing, reviewing, and editing. In the editing process, trim excess words from sentences such as piled-up modifiers, from excessive use of prepositions, and the "the . . . of" constructions (e.g., "the study of") that add unnecessary verbiage to a study (Ross-Larson, 1982). I was reminded of the unnecessary prose that comes into writing by the example mentioned by Bunge (1985):

Nowadays you can almost see bright people struggling to reinvent the complex sentence before your eyes. A friend of mine who is a college administrator every now and then has to say a complex sentence, and he will get into one of those morasses that begins, "I would hope that we would be able . . ." He never talked that way when I first met him, but even at his age, at his distance from the crisis in the lives of younger people, he's been to some extent alienated from easy speech. (Bunge, 1985, p. 172)

Begin studying good writing that uses both qualitative and quantitative designs. In good writing the eye does not pause and the mind stumble on a passage. In this book I have attempted to draw examples of good prose from human and social science journals such as the *American Journal of Sociology, The American Cartographer, Journal of Applied Psychology, Administrative Science Quarterly, American Educational Research Journal, Sociology of Education,* and *IMAGE: Journal of Nursing Scholarship.* In the qualitative area, good literature serves to illustrate clear prose and detailed passages. Individuals who teach qualitative research assign classical literature such as *Moby Dick, The Scarlet Letter,* and *The Bonfire of the Vanities* as reading assignments in qualitative courses (Webb & Glesne, 1992).

## COMPUTER PROGRAMS FOR WRITING

Word processing programs come with built-in spelling checkers and thesaurus programs. Look for an advanced professional word processing program that contains these features. Phrase-checking computer software programs also help writers edit their prose. For example, **Correct Grammar** (Lifetree Software, Inc., 1989) provides an advanced-level phrase-checking program that looks for 1,400 flaws in writing. These flaws include spelling and format (e.g., idiomatic expressions), sentences (e.g., fragments and passive constructions), usage (e.g., wordy expressions such as "a half a"), and grammar (e.g., subject-verb agreement).

▼ *After constructing a proposal or a study, enter it into a program such as* **Correct Grammar.** The program not only will highlight the mistakes but also will provide suggestions for improvement.

## SUMMARY

In this chapter I reviewed writing techniques helpful in designing research studies. Consider good writing techniques early in the research process and use the process of writing to think through ideas. The thought process continues through successive drafts of a plan, and it might begin with designing a general outline, writing out ideas and restructuring entire paragraphs, and finally editing the prose. This process requires the discipline and habit of writing: a continual process of working in small, regular amounts. The process might begin each day with "warm-up" exercises and be enhanced by favorite implements of writing and a location conducive to disciplined thought.

The manuscript needs to read smoothly and easily, and I recommend building coherence into the draft by using consistent terms and attending to narrative "thoughts"—the umbrella, big, little, and attention or interest thoughts. Coherence builds, too, through good connecting sentences and paragraphs.

At the micro level, writers emphasize the importance of using the active voice, strong action verbs, a verb tense appropriate for the audience, and trimming the "fat" from sentences through eliminating piled-up modifiers, excessive prepositions, and wordy phrases such as "the study of . . ." Reading good research helps one see strong prose, and one can be aided in the writing process by computer software programs that check phrases, wordiness, and grammatical mistakes.

## WRITING EXERCISES

1. Describe your "warm-up" exercises. Try some of the activities recommended in this chapter.

2. Write a proposal for a scholarly study. Begin by developing a general outline, writing a first draft, shifting paragraphs around, and editing the copy.

3. Keep a daily chart of your writing during the process of developing a plan for a study. Indicate (a) time spent on writing, (b) page equivalents finished, (c) percentage of planned task completed, and (d) the next task to be completed.

4. Examine the introduction to your proposed study that you were asked to develop during the writing exercise for Chapter 3. Using the "hook and eye" technique, connect major thoughts from sentence to sentence and paragraph to paragraph. Indicate where you need to edit transitions into the manuscript.

5. Start a journal that you keep during the process of writing your research plan. As you edit your prose, write down problem phrases, prepositions, piled-up modifiers, and wordy phrases. Enter the problems uncovered into a computer check of your prose.

# ▼ ADDITIONAL READINGS

Bailey, E. P. (1984). **Writing clearly: A contemporary approach.**
Columbus, OH: Charles E. Merrill.

> Edward Bailey writes about a new style of writing based on the
> principles of clear and easy writing. In the first section of his book,
> Bailey describes contemporary views on research about language,
> writing, and reading. For example, in the section on contemporary
> views on writing, he discusses writing as a recursive process of
> prewriting, writing, and rewriting and talks about writing as think-
> ing, the role of the unconscious, finding one's voice, and speaking
> to an audience. In the second part of this book, Bailey presents a
> "new style" of writing consistent with contemporary views. Informal
> writing, use of simple words, a natural word order, conciseness, "road
> signs," and sentence structure form his core ideas. Especially useful
> is the section on "road signs," the use of transitional words and phrases.
> He presents lists of conjunctive adverbs (e.g., *accordingly*), coordi-
> nating conjunctions (e.g., *yet*), and subordinating conjunctions (e.g.,
> *although*) that should be handy lists at the fingertips of scholars.

Carroll, D. L. (1990). **A manual of writer's tricks.** New York:
Paragon House.

> David Carroll's "tricks" consist of pieces of hard-won and valuable
> advice about how to write and how to write better. The book covers
> vocabulary, tone, expression, style, structure, and rewriting and
> correcting. A section is presented on exercises to build writing skills.
> Emphasis throughout is on the need to understand the details of the
> writing craft. Each point is illustrated with examples from well-
> known writers. Best of all, each "tried-and-true trick" in Carroll's
> book really works.

Goldberg, N. (1986). **Writing down the bones: Freeing the writer
within.** Boston: Shambhala.

Goldberg, N. (1990). **Wild mind: Living the writer's life.** New
York: Bantam Books.

Natalie Goldberg's two very readable books provide a Zen orientation on writing. They focus on the detailed craft of the writer and provide many memorable accounts of how to develop particular techniques and skills. As well, Goldberg is interested in the physical, social, and psychological dimensions of writing and offers much practical advice on how to survive the often stressful and demanding role of the writer. She suggests that writing is a lonely task during which one is compelled to pare down the words until they say exactly what one wants them to say: no more and no less.

Madsen, D. (1990). **Successful dissertations and theses.** San Francisco: Jossey-Bass.

In Chapter 6 David Madsen provides practical advice on the vital preliminary step of outlining the narrative of a piece of completed research. He presents examples of both topic and sentence outlines. Emphasis is placed on the importance of structure in writing and therefore on the need to develop clear organizational principles. Such principles might emphasize chronology (in historical research) or cause and effect (an experimental study). Further attention is paid to the writing of drafts (with examples of both "wordy" and "tightened" passages) and to the preparation of the abstract and the typing of the final copy.

Richardson, L. (1990). **Writing strategies: Reaching diverse audiences.** Newbury Park, CA: Sage.

Laurel Richardson's book, published in a series dealing with qualitative research methods, contains a section dealing with the use of quotations in narrative. Short quotations, embedded quotations, and longer quotations are all discussed. Richardson also devotes a chapter to writing academic papers. She emphasizes the malleability of qualitative research data; the final product will be the result of many decisions made by the writer. Particular attention is paid to narrative stance and other rhetorical devices through which the writer can shape the material to make it appropriate for its intended audience.

Tarshis, B. (1982). **How to write like a pro: A guide to effective nonfiction writing.** New York: New American Library.

Barry Tarshis is an experienced writer who shares his ideas and talents. His emphasis is on the readability of writing. He stresses the importance of style and structure as a means of ensuring the reader's attention. Many examples of both good and bad writing are analyzed in detail. Included are pithy sections on "lazy" verbs and "fat" writing. Tarshis will help scholars make their research more readable.

# References

American Psychological Association (APA). (1984). *Publication manual of the American Psychological Association* (3rd ed.). Washington, DC: Author.

Anderson, B. F. (1971). *The psychology experiment: An introduction to the scientific method.* Belmont, CA: Brooks/Cole.

Armstrong, R. L. (1974). Hypotheses: Why? When? How? *Phi Delta Kappan, 54,* 213-214.

Babbie, E. (1990). *Survey research methods* (2nd ed.). Belmont, CA: Wadsworth.

Bailey, E. P. (1984). *Writing clearly: A contemporary approach.* Columbus, OH: Charles E. Merrill.

Bean, J., & Creswell, J. W. (1980). Student attrition among women at a liberal arts college. *Journal of College Student Personnel, 3,* 320-327.

Beisel, N. (1990, February). Class, culture, and campaigns against vice in three American cities, 1872-1892. *American Sociological Review, 55,* 44-62.

Bem, D. (1987). Writing the empirical journal article. In M. P. Zanna & J. M. Darley (Eds.), *The compleat academic: A practical guide for the beginning social scientist* (pp. 171-201). New York: Random House.

Blalock, H. (1969). *Theory construction: From verbal to mathematical formulations.* Englewood Cliffs, NJ: Prentice Hall.

Blalock, H. (1985). *Causal models in the social sciences.* Hawthorne, NY: Aldine.

Blase, J. J. (1989). The micropolitics of the school: The everyday political orientation of teachers toward open school principals. *Educational Administration Quarterly, 25*(4), 379-409.

Boeker, W. (1992). Power and managerial dismissal: Scapegoating at the top. *Administrative Science Quarterly, 37,* 400-421.

Bogdan, R. C., & Biklen, S. K. (1992). *Qualitative research for education: An introduction to theory and methods.* Boston: Allyn & Bacon.

Boice, R. (1990). *Professors as writers: A self-help guide to productive writing.* Stillwater, OK: New Forums.

Booth-Kewley, S., Edwards, J. E., & Rosenfeld, P. (1992). Impression management, social desirability, and computer administration of attitude questionnaires: Does the computer make a difference? *Journal of Applied Psychology, 77*(4), 562-566.

Borg, W. R., Gall, J. P., & Gall, M. D. (1993). *Applying educational research: A practical guide* (3rd ed.). White Plains, NY: Longman.

Borg, W. R., & Gall, M. D. (1989). *Educational research: An introduction* (5th ed.). New York: Longman.

Brewer, J., & Hunter, A. (1989). *Multimethod research: A synthesis of styles.* Newbury Park, CA: Sage.

Brooks, C., & Warren, R. P. (1961). *Modern rhetoric: Shorter edition.* New York: Harcourt, Brace & World.

Bunge, N. (1985). *Finding the words: Conversations with writers who teach.* Athens: Ohio University Press.

Cahill, S. E. (1989). Fashioning males and females: Appearance management and the social reproduction of gender. *Symbolic Interaction, 12*(2), 281-298.

Campbell, D. T., & Fiske, D. (1959). Convergent and discriminant validation by the multitrait-multimethod matrix. *Psychological Bulletin, 56,* 81-105.

Campbell, D. T., & Stanley, J. C. (1966). Experimental and quasi-experimental designs for research. In N. L. Gage (Ed.), *Handbook of research on teaching* (pp. 1-76). Chicago: Rand McNally.

Campbell, W. G., & Ballou, S. V. (1977). *Form and style: Theses, reports, term papers* (5th ed.). Boston: Houghton Mifflin.

Carroll, D. L. (1990). *A manual of writer's tricks.* New York: Paragon House.

Carstensen, L. W., Jr. (1989). A fractal analysis of cartographic generalization. *American Cartographer, 16*(3), 181-189.

Castetter, W. B., & Heisler, R. S. (1977). *Developing and defending a dissertation proposal.* Philadelphia: University of Pennsylvania, Graduate School of Education, Center for Field Studies.

Cohen, J. (1977). *Statistical power analysis for the behavioral sciences.* New York: Academic Press.

Conrad, C. F. (1978, April). A grounded theory of academic change. *Sociology of Education, 51,* 101-112.

Cook, T. D., & Campbell, D. T. (1979). *Quasi experimentation: Design and analysis issues for field settings.* Chicago: Rand McNally.

Cooper, H. (1984). *The integrative research review: A systematic approach.* Beverly Hills, CA: Sage.

Creswell, J. W., & Brown, M. L. (1992). How chairpersons enhance faculty research: A grounded theory study. *The Review of Higher Education, 16*(1), 41-62.

Creswell, J. W., Seagren, A., & Henry, T. (1979). Professional development training needs of department chairpersons: A test of the Biglan model. *Planning and Changing, 10,* 224-237.

Crutchfield, J. P. (1986). *Locus of control, interpersonal trust, and scholarly productivity.* Unpublished doctoral dissertation, University of Nebraska, Lincoln.

DeGraw, D. G. (1984). *Job motivational factors of educators within adult correctional institutions from various states.* Unpublished doctoral dissertation, University of Nebraska, Lincoln.

Denzin, N. K. (1978). *The research act: A theoretical introduction to sociological methods* (2nd ed.). New York: McGraw-Hill.

Dillard, A. (1989). *The writing life.* New York: Harper & Row.

Dillman, D. A. (1978). *Mail and telephone surveys: The total design method.* New York: John Wiley.

Drew, N. (1986). Exclusion and confirmation: A phenomenology of patients' experiences with caregivers. *IMAGE: Journal of Nursing Scholarship, 18*(2), 39-43.

DuBois, L. (1986). *The structure of clinical science instruction in colleges of dentistry.* Unpublished doctoral dissertation, University of Nebraska, Lincoln.

Dukes, S. (1984). Phenomenological methodology in the human sciences. *Journal of Religion and Health, 23*(3), 197-203.

Duncan, O. D. (1985). Path analysis: Sociological examples. In H. M. Blalock, Jr. (Ed.), *Causal models in the social sciences* (2nd ed., pp. 55-79). Hawthorne, NY: Aldine.

Educational Resources Information Center (ERIC). (1969-). *Current index to journals in education.* New York: Macmillan.

Educational Resources Information Center (ERIC). (1975). *Thesaurus of ERIC descriptors* (12th ed.). Phoenix, AZ: Oryx.

Educational Resources Information Center (ERIC). (1975-). *Resources in education.* Washington, DC: U.S. Department of Health, Education, and Welfare.

Eisner, E. W. (1991). *The enlightened eye: Qualitative inquiry and the enhancement of educational practice.* New York: Macmillan.

Elbow, P. (1973). *Writing without teachers.* London: Oxford University Press.

Enns, C. Z., & Hackett, G. (1990). Comparison of feminist and nonfeminist women's reactions to variants of nonsexist and feminist counseling. *Journal of Counseling Psychology, 37*(1), 33-40.

Erlandson, D. A., Harris, E. L., Skipper, B. L., & Allen, S. D. (1993). *Doing naturalistic inquiry: A guide to methods.* Newbury Park, CA: Sage.

Fetterman, D. M. (1989). *Ethnography: Step by step.* Newbury Park, CA: Sage.

Field, P. A., & Morse, J. M. (1985). *Qualitative nursing research: The application of qualitative approaches.* Rockville, MD: Aspen.

Fielding, N. G., & Lee, R. M. (1991). *Using computers in qualitative research.* Newbury Park, CA: Sage.

Fink, A., & Kosecoff, J. (1985). *How to conduct surveys: A step-by-step guide.* Beverly Hills, CA: Sage.

Finlay, M., & Mitchell, J. (1991). *The CD-ROM directory, 1992* (7th ed.). London: TFPL.

Firestone, W. A. (1987). Meaning in method: The rhetoric of quantitative and qualitative research. *Educational Researcher, 16*(7), 16-21.

Fowler, F. J. (1988). *Survey research methods.* Newbury Park, CA: Sage.

Fraenkel, J. R., & Wallen, N. E. (1990). *How to design and evaluate research in education.* New York: McGraw-Hill.

Franklin, J. (1986). *Writing for story: Craft secrets of dramatic nonfiction by a two-time Pulitzer prize-winner.* New York: Atheneum.

Gioia, D. A., & Pitre, E. (1990). Multiparadigm perspectives on theory building. *Academy of Management Review, 15*(4), 584-602.

Glaser, B. (1978). *Theoretical sensitivity.* Mill Valley, CA: Sociology Press.

Goetz, J. P., & LeCompte, M. D. (1984). *Ethnography and qualitative design in educational research.* New York: Academic Press.

Gogolin, L., & Swartz, F. (1992). A quantitative and qualitative inquiry into the attitudes toward science of nonscience college students. *Journal of Research in Science Teaching, 29*(5), 487-504.

Goldberg, N. (1986). *Writing down the bones: Freeing the writer within.* Boston: Shambhala.

Goldberg, N. (1990). *Wild mind: Living the writer's life.* New York: Bantam.

Goodman, J., & Adler, S. (1985). Becoming an elementary social studies teacher: A study of perspectives. *Theory and Research in Social Education, XIII*(2), 1-20.

Grant, L., & Fine, G. A. (1992). Sociology unleashed: Creative directions in classical ethnography. In M. D. LeCompte, W. L. Millroy, & J. Preissle (Eds.), *The handbook of qualitative research in education* (pp. 405-446). New York: Academic Press.

Greene, J. C., Caracelli, V. J., & Graham, W. F. (1989). Toward a conceptual framework for mixed-method evaluation designs. *Educational Evaluation and Policy Analysis, 11*(3), 255-274.

Guba, E. (1992). *The paradigm dialog.* Newbury Park, CA: Sage.

Guba, E. G., & Lincoln, Y. (1988). Do inquiry paradigms imply inquiry methodologies? In D. M. Fetterman (Ed.), *Qualitative approaches to evaluation in education* (pp. 89-115). New York: Praeger.

Hodges, J. C., & Whitten, M. E. (1977). *Harbrace college handbook* (8th ed.). Orlando, FL: Harcourt Brace Jovanovich.

Hofstede, G., Neuijen, B., Ohayv, D. D., & Sanders, G. (1990). Measuring organizational cultures: A qualitative and quantitative study across twenty cases. *Administrative Science Quarterly, 35,* 286-316.

Homans, G. C. (1950). *The human group.* New York: Harcourt, Brace.

Hopkins, T. K. (1964). *The exercise of influence in small groups.* Totowa, NJ: Bedmister.

Howe, K., & Eisenhart, M. (1990). Standards for qualitative (and quantitative) research: A prolegomenon. *Educational Researcher, 19*(4), 2-9.

Institute for Scientific Information. (1969-). *Social sciences citation index.* Philadelphia: Author.

Isaac, S., & Michael, W. B. (1981). *Handbook in research and evaluation: A collection of principles, methods, and strategies useful in the planning, design, and evaluation of studies in education and the behavioral sciences* (2nd ed.). San Diego: EdITS.

Jacob, E. (1987). Qualitative research traditions: A review. *Review of Educational Research, 57*(1), 1-50.

Jick, T. D. (1979, December). Mixing qualitative and quantitative methods: Triangulation in action. *Administrative Science Quarterly, 24,* 602-611.

Jungnickel, P. W. (1990). *Workplace correlates and scholarly performance of pharmacy clinical faculty members.* Unpublished dissertation proposal, University of Nebraska, Lincoln.

Keppel, G. (1991). *Design and analysis: A researcher's handbook* (3rd ed.). Englewood Cliffs, NJ: Prentice Hall.

Kerlinger, F. N. (1973). *Foundations of behavioral research.* New York: Holt, Rinehart & Winston.

Kerlinger, F. N. (1979). *Behavioral research: A conceptual approach.* New York: Holt, Rinehart & Winston.

Kos, R. (1991). Persistence of reading disabilities: The voices of four middle school students. *American Educational Research Journal, 28*(4), 875-895.

Krathwohl, D. R. (1987). *Social and behavioral science research: A new framework for conceptualizing, implementing, and evaluating research studies.* San Francisco: Jossey-Bass.

Krathwohl, D. R. (1988). *How to prepare a research proposal: Guidelines for funding and dissertations in the social and behavioral sciences.* Syracuse, NY: Syracuse University Press.

Krol, E. (1993). *The whole Internet: User's guide and catalog.* Sebastopol, CA: O'Reilly & Associates.

Kuhn, T. (1970). *The structure of scientific revolutions.* Chicago: University of Chicago Press.

Kunes, M. V. (1991). *How the workplace affects the self-esteem of the psychiatric nurse.* Unpublished dissertation proposal. University of Nebraska, Lincoln.

Kushman, J. W. (1992). The organizational dynamics of teacher workplace. *Educational Administration Quarterly, 28*(1), 5-42.

Labovitz, S., & Hagedorn, R. (1971). *Introduction to social research.* New York: McGraw-Hill.

Lancy, D. F. (1993). *Qualitative research in education: An introduction to the major traditions.* New York: Longman.

LaQuey, T. L. (1993). *The Internet companion: A beginner's guide to global networking.* Reading, MA: Addison-Wesley.

Lather, P. (1986). Research as praxis. *Harvard Educational Review, 56,* 257-277.

Leslie, L. L. (1972). Are high response rates essential to valid surveys? *Social Science Research, 1,* 323-334.

Lifetree Software, Inc. (1989). *Correct grammar: For IBM personal computers and compatibles* [Computer program]. San Francisco: Author.

Lincoln, Y. S., & Guba, E. G. (1985). *Naturalistic inquiry.* Beverly Hills, CA: Sage.

Locke, L. F., Spirduso, W. W., & Silverman, S. J. (1987). *Proposals that work: A guide for planning dissertations and grant proposals* (2nd ed.). Newbury Park, CA: Sage.

Locke, W. (1991). *Nebraska's outdoor education programs.* Unpublished proposal, University of Nebraska, Lincoln.

Madsen, D. (1990). *Successful dissertations and theses.* San Francisco: Jossey-Bass.

Mandell, N. (1984). Children's negotiation of meaning. *Symbolic Interaction, 7*(3), 191-211.

Marshall, C., & Rossman, G. B. (1989). *Designing qualitative research.* Newbury Park, CA: Sage.

Mascarenhas, B. (1989). Domains of state-owned, privately held, and publicly traded firms in international competition. *Administrative Science Quarterly, 34,* 582-597.

Mason, E. J., & Bramble, W. J. (1989). *Understanding and conducting research: Applications in education and the behavioral sciences.* New York: McGraw-Hill.

Mathison, S. (1988). Why triangulate? *Educational Researcher, 17*(2), 13-17.

McCracken, G. (1988). *The long interview.* Newbury Park, CA: Sage.

McMillan, J. H., & Schumacher, S. (1989). *Research in education: A conceptual introduction.* New York: HarperCollins.

Megel, M. E., Langston, N. F., & Creswell, J. W. (1988). Scholarly productivity: A survey of nursing faculty researchers. *Journal of Professional Nursing, 4,* 45-54.

Merriam, S. B. (1988). *Case study research in education: A qualitative approach.* San Francisco: Jossey-Bass.

Miles, M. B., & Huberman, A. M. (1984). *Qualitative data analysis: A sourcebook of new methods.* Beverly Hills, CA: Sage.

Miller, D. (1992). *The experiences of a first-year college president: An ethnography.* Unpublished doctoral dissertation proposal, University of Nebraska, Lincoln.

Miller, D. C. (1991). *Handbook of research design and social measurement* (5th ed.). Newbury Park, CA: Sage.

Mitchell, M., & Saunders, L. M. (1991, April). The virtual library: An agenda for the 1990s. *Computers in Libraries,* pp. 8-11.

Moore, G. W. (1983). *Developing and evaluating educational research.* Boston: Little, Brown.

Morse, J. M. (1991). Approaches to qualitative-quantitative methodological triangulation. *Nursing Research, 40*(1), 120-123.

Murguia, E., Padilla, R. V., & Pavel, M. (1991, September). Ethnicity and the concept of social integration in Tinto's model of institutional departure. *Journal of College Student Development, 32,* 433-439.

Neuman, W. L. (1991). *Social research methods: Qualitative and quantitative approaches.* Boston: Allyn & Bacon.

Nieswiadomy, R. M. (1993). *Foundations of nursing research* (2nd ed.). Norwalk, CT: Appleton & Lange.

Oberon Resources. (1990). *WP citation.* Columbus, OH: Author.

Oiler, C. J. (1986). Phenomenology: The method. In P. L. Munhall & C. J. Oiler (Eds.), *Nursing research: A qualitative perspective* (pp. 69-83). New York: Appleton-Century-Crofts.

Patton, M. J. (1991, September). Qualitative research on college students: Philosophical and methodological comparisons with the quantitative approach. *Journal of College Student Development, 32,* 389-396.

Patton, M. Q. (1980). *Qualitative research methods.* Beverly Hills, CA: Sage.

Patton, M. Q. (1988). Paradigms and pragmatism. In D. M. Fetterman (Ed.), *Qualitative approaches to evaluation in education* (pp. 116-137). New York: Praeger.

Phillips, D. C. (1987). *Philosophy, science, and social inquiry: Contemporary methodological controversies in social science and related applied fields of research.* Elmsford, NY: Pergamon.

Polyson, J., Levinson, M., & Miller, H. (1982). Writing styles: A survey of psychology journal editors. *American Psychologist, 37,* 335-338.

Price, J. L., & Mueller, C. W. (1986). *Handbook of organizational measurement.* New York: Longman.

Quantz, R. A. (1992). On critical ethnography (with some postmodern considerations). In M. D. LeCompte, W. L. Millroy, & J. Preissle (Eds.), *The handbook of qualitative research in education* (pp. 447-505). New York: Academic Press.

Reichardt, C. S., & Cook, T. D. (1979). Beyond qualitative versus quantitative methods. In T. D. Cook & C. S. Reichardt (Eds.), *Qualitative and quantitative methods in evaluation research* (pp. 7-32). Beverly Hills, CA: Sage.

Richardson, L. (1990). *Writing strategies: Reaching diverse audiences.* Newbury Park, CA: Sage.

Riemen, D. J. (1986). The essential structure of a caring interaction: Doing phenomenology. In P. M. Munhall & C. J. Oiler (Eds.), *Nursing research: A qualitative perspective* (pp. 85-108). New York: Appleton-Century-Crofts.

Rosenthal, R., & Rosnow, R. L. (1991). *Essentials of behavioral research: Methods and data analysis* (2nd ed.). New York: McGraw-Hill.

Ross-Larson, B. (1982). *Edit yourself: A manual for everyone who works with words.* New York: Norton.

Rossman, G. B., & Wilson, B. L. (1985). Numbers and words: Combining quantitative and qualitative methods in a single large-scale evaluation study. *Evaluation Review, 9*(5), 627-643.

Rudestam, K. E., & Newton, R. R. (1992). *Surviving your dissertation.* Newbury Park, CA: Sage.

Salkind, N. (1990). *Exploring research.* New York: Macmillan.

Salomon, G. (1991). Transcending the qualitative-quantitative debate: The analytic and systemic approaches to educational research. *Educational Researcher, 20*(6), 10-18.

Schuyler, M. (1992). *Dial in 1992: An annual guide to online public access catalogs.* Westport, CT: Meckler.

Sheehy, E. P. (Ed.). (1986). *Guide to reference books* (10th ed.). Chicago: American Library Association.

Smith, J. K. (1983, March). Quantitative versus qualitative research: An attempt to clarify the issue. *Educational Researcher,* pp. 6-13.

Smith, M. L. (1987). Publishing qualitative research. *American Educational Research Journal, 24*(2), 173-183.

Spradley, J. P. (1979). *The ethnographic interview.* Fort Worth, TX: Harcourt Brace Jovanovich College Publishers.

Spradley, J. P. (1980). *Participant observation.* New York: Holt, Rinehart & Winston.

Steinbeck, J. (1969). *Journal of a novel: The East of Eden letters.* New York: Viking.

Stock, M. (1985). *A practical guide to graduate research.* New York: McGraw-Hill.

Strauss, A., & Corbin, J. (1990). *Basics of qualitative research: Grounded theory procedures and techniques.* Newbury Park, CA: Sage.

Sudduth, A. G. (1992). *Rural hospitals' use of strategic adaptation in a changing health care environment.* Unpublished doctoral dissertation, University of Nebraska, Lincoln.

Sudman, S., & Bradburn, N. M. (1986). *Asking questions.* San Francisco: Jossey-Bass.

Swanson, S. (1992, April). *Mixed-method triangulation: Theory and practice compared.* Paper presented at the Annual Meeting of the American Educational Research Association, San Francisco.

Tarshis, B. (1982). *How to write like a pro: A guide to effective nonfiction writing.* New York: New American Library.

Tenopir, C., & Neufang, R. (1992, March). Electronic reference options: How they stack up in research libraries. *Online,* pp. 22-28.

Terenzini, P. T., Pascarella, E. T., & Lorang, W. G. (1982). An assessment of the academic and social influences on freshman year educational outcomes. *The Review of Higher Education, 5*(2), 86-109.

Tesch, R. (1990). *Qualitative research: Analysis types and software tools.* New York: Falmer.

Thomas, J. (1993). *Doing critical ethnography.* Newbury Park, CA: Sage.

Tuckman, B. (1990). A proposal for improving the quality of published educational research. *Educational Researcher, 19*(9), 22-25.

Turabian, K. L. (1973). *A manual for writers of term papers, theses, and dissertations* (4th ed.). Chicago: University of Chicago Press.

University Microfilms. (1938-). *Dissertation abstracts international.* Ann Arbor, MI: Author.

University of Chicago Press. (1993). *The Chicago manual of style* (14th ed.). Chicago: Author.

Van Maanen, J. (1981). The informant game: Selected aspects of ethnographic research in police organizations. *Urban Life, 9*(4), 469-494.

Van Maanen, J. (1988). *Tales of the field: On writing ethnography.* Chicago: University of Chicago Press.

Vernon, J. E. (1992). *The impact of divorce on the grandparent-grandchild relationship when the parent generation divorces.* Unpublished doctoral dissertation, University of Nebraska, Lincoln.

Wallen, N. E., & Fraenkel, J. R. (1991). *Educational research: A guide to the process.* New York: McGraw-Hill.

Webb, R. B., & Glesne, C. (1992). Teaching qualitative research. In M. D. LeCompte, W. L. Millroy, & J. Preissle (Eds.), *The handbook of qualitative research in education* (pp. 771-814). New York: Academic Press.

Webb, W. H., Beals, A. R., & White, C. M. (1986). *Sources of information in the social sciences: A guide to the literature* (3rd ed.). Chicago: American Library Association.

Werner, O., & Schoepfle, G. (1987). *Systematic fieldwork: Vol. 1, Foundations of ethnography and interviewing.* Newbury Park, CA: Sage.

Wilkinson, A. M. (1991). *The scientist's handbook for writing papers and dissertations.* Englewood Cliffs, NJ: Prentice Hall.

Wittstruck, G. (1986). *Myers-Briggs type indicator and leadership effectiveness in student affairs.* Unpublished doctoral dissertation, University of Nebraska, Lincoln.

Wolcott, H. T. (1990). *Writing up qualitative research.* Newbury Park, CA: Sage.

WordPerfect Corporation. (1989). *WordPerfect 5.1* [Computer program]. Orem, UT: Author.

Yin, R. K. (1989). *Case study research: Design and methods.* Newbury Park, CA: Sage.

Ziller, R. C. (1990). *Photographing the self: Methods for observing personal orientations.* Newbury Park, CA: Sage.

Zinsser, W. (1983). *Writing with a word processor.* New York: Harper Colophon.

# Author Index

# Subject Index

▼

# *About the Author*

John W. Creswell is a Professor of Educational Psychology at Teachers College, University of Nebraska, Lincoln. He specializes in qualitative and quantitative research designs and methods, as well as faculty and academic leadership issues in colleges and universities. He has authored four books—two on faculty research performance and two on the academic leadership of department chairpersons. Widely published in national journals, he has served on numerous editorial boards for educational journals and currently holds the position of Associate Editor for *The Review of Higher Education*. He lives in Lincoln, Nebraska, with his wife and two teenage children.